Marvellous Méliès

KU-112-332

PAUL HAMMOND

Marvellous Méliès

GORDON FRASER · LONDON 1974

First published 1974 by
The Gordon Fraser Gallery Ltd., London and Bedford

Advisory editor Michael Wallington
Copyright © Paul Hammond 1974
ISBN 0 900406 38 0 hardcover
ISBN 0 900406 39 9 softcover
The softcover edition is sold subject to the condition
that it shall not, by way of trade or otherwise, be
lent, re-sold, hired out or otherwise circulated,
without the publisher's prior consent, in any form
of binding or cover other than that in which it is
published, and without a similar condition including
these words being imposed on a subsequent
purchaser.

HERTFORDSHIRE
COUNTY LIBRARY

902683

791.43

Printed in Great Britain by
Fletcher & Son Ltd, Norwich
Designed by Peter Guy

Contents

Darkened Rooms   7

Life and Work (1861–1938)   13

Star Film Critique   87

The Writing on the Wall   127

APPENDIX I: References   131

APPENDIX II: Georges Méliès Trickography   135

APPENDIX III: Georges Méliès Filmography   137

APPENDIX IV: Gaston Méliès Filmography   153

For consummate Christine

ACKNOWLEDGEMENTS
The author would like to thank the following people, all of whom helped in the preparation of this book:
Gerald Ashford; John Barnes of The Barnes Museum of Cinematography, St Ives, Cornwall; Jeremy Boulton of the National Film Archive, London; Suzanne Budgen; Rudy Burckhardt; Jacques Deslandes; James Fraser; Patrick Hughes; George A. Jenness; Madeleine Malthête-Méliès of Les Amis de Georges Méliès, Paris; Hans Richter; Patrick J. Sheehan of the Motion Picture Section, Library of Congress, Washington DC; Mike Wallington; W. J. Webb of the Fairground Society.

PICTURE CREDITS
The illustrations came from the collections of:
John Barnes; Rudy Burckhardt; Jacques Deslandes; the Fairground Society; George Jenness; Kemp R. Niver Collection, Library of Congress; Madeleine Malthête-Méliès and S.P.A.D.E.M.; the Museum of Modern Art, New York; the National Film Archive; the Science Museum, London; the Walker Art Gallery, Liverpool.

Darkened Rooms

"The cinema? Three cheers for darkened rooms."
—André Breton

It is well known that the cinema has its origins in optical toys and amusements like Plateau's Phenakistiscope and Reynaud's Praxinoscope and in the photography of movement, especially Marey's chronophotographs. It is less well known that the cinema also has its roots in the theatre of spectacle, in forms like the pantomime and comic-opera, music-hall and conjuring shows. The main feature of conjuring and magic theatre, which began to flourish in the 1860s, was the exploitation of optical trickery to achieve spectacular imagery, with isolated illusions linked by melodramatic narrative. The appeal of magic was partly to be found in its thrilling coalition of polarities, and their careful manipulation to

Pantomime and magic in the early cinema. A punch turns a white clown into a lunatic Negro in *Off to Bloomingdale Asylum* (1901).

induce alternate feelings of well-being and disorientation in the spectator. The emotive use of darkness and light (that is, the illusory secrecy of black on black and the drama and clarity of white on black) underlines the extreme and dynamic nature of this kind of entertainment.

The 500 films that Georges Méliès made between 1896 and 1912 include conjuring turns, burlesques, reconstructed newsreels, melodramas, fantastic voyages, stag films, fairy stories, satires, costume dramas, literary adaptations and advertising films. All were in some sense theatrical and spectacular—his experience as a conjuror, his delirious imagination and his inherited wealth combined to offer him superior opportunities to develop the trick potential of moving images.

It is current critical canon to see Méliès as an engaging primitive whose work has mere historical and curiosity value. The viewpoint of this book is very different. Méliès has the greatest contemporary significance. Whereas most critics hold his conception of cinema to be obsolete, we would suggest, paradoxically, that it incorporates a viable approach to all film. Méliès thought of his films as connected fragments, and he compared his rôle to the compère of a revue who "is there to link the acts that have nothing to do with each other".[1] The spectacular irruption of cathartic imagery within a secondary narrative is central to Méliès' aesthetic. His films make the viewer aware of the validity of the heightened, autonomous image. The independence of the isolated image and its ability to shock and astound has implications for any critical conception of the cinema.

In studying Méliès' films, in handling them, we tend to read them as solitary images, or rather as pairs of images, for it is particularly intriguing to scrutinise the adjacent frames that depict a trick transformation. These adjacent images are the focal points of his work. This kind of intimate contact makes Stan Brakhage's words most apposite: "I took my first senses of the individual frame life of a film from Méliès."[2] Of the 500 films Méliès made, less than 90 have survived. Some of the lost films exist as single images only, as stills or sketches. We must treat these images as the meaningful residue of the lost work. His use of painted sets during shooting and the hand-colouring of individual frames in the laboratory indicate that Méliès used almost wholly graphic means to conceptualise his works. His films have their inspiration and reference as much in painting, illustration and caricature, in static images and set pieces, as in anything

else. And the situation of the autonomous image touches
upon the issue of filmic memory and discourse, the way we remember films and the way we talk about them. Every book on the cinema contains, as this one does, *stills*, a few of them taken from the frame itself, but most made with a still-camera during (or even before and after) production.

So, far from being a quaint precursor, Méliès can teach us, if we pay him enough attention, how to look at films. From him we can learn to consider the cinema as a medium animated by marvellous moments owing little allegiance to the banal narrative structures that hold them prisoner. From Méliès we can elucidate a structure of the cinema that consists of revelatory and cathartic images liberated from their obligations to good sense. These images might be thought of as 'shots' in a purely mental film of which we are each at best the director or at worst the continuity-girl. The intention must be to create an ever more complex web of *emblems* "to be lived directly".[3] While an image exists to be interpreted it also exists to be experienced for itself, in an occult sort of way. Although never scornful of theorising, it is the primacy of the image that we must hold dear. Méliès will repay us by verifying, even radicalising, that conception.

Marvellous is the word we have used to describe Méliès' films. "The marvellous," said André Breton, "has never been better defined than as being in complete contrast to the fantastic."[4] This antithesis is worth considering, for it sheds light on the whole structure and development of the so-called fantasy film, a genre that has its first mentor in Méliès.

The *marvellous* (le merveilleux) indicates an harmonious, parallel world, whereas the *fantastic* (le fantastique) refers to the shock experienced when abnormal, monstrous forces emerge to disrupt the equilibrium of normal, everyday reality. The imaginary irrupts into the real and thereby puts reality on trial. The marvellous presents us with the impossible happening in a world where impossibility is the rule, while the fantastic presents us with the impossible happening in a world where impossibility is outlawed. The fantastic seems to emerge in the eighteenth century because a scientific conception of the world began to predominate: the more the universe was rationalised the greater heights the Romantic imagination reached. The marvellous, on the other hand, existed long before this period; indeed, it informs any number of myths. That the marvellous flourished in the early cinema, we have Méliès' films as testament. According to Gérard Lenne,[5] it was the arrival of sound that largely laid the marvellous to rest since the talkie re-established the audio-visual duality of everyday life, thereby encouraging a stronger fantastic strain to emerge. The more 'real' the depiction of reality is, the more profound its sub-version by the imaginary becomes. It is logical to assume, then, that the silent cinema's very limitations, the fact that it was silent, obliged it to turn to the marvellous in the early days.

Méliès' career in films may also have ended because the cinema ceased to be an artisanal enterprise predicated often on anti-realist assumptions, and became capitalistic with increasing realism as its prevailing mode of representation. Like the economic stage which spawned them, Méliès' films disappeared, so that today less than one-sixth of his œuvre exists. Méliès considered his own work to be of no cultural value: he personally put a match to a stockpile of his films. It was not until the late 1920s that the first real historians of the cinema began to study the pioneers and by that time much material had been destroyed.

Marvellous Méliès is the first book in English on the subject and we regard it as the most accurate in any language. Maurice Bessy and G. M. Lo Duca's *Georges Méliès, mage*[6] contains abundant illustrations and a variety of documents, including *Mes Mémoires* which, written at the end of Méliès' life, are responsible for many of the errors which have become part of the Méliès legend. Maurice Bessy's pamphlet, *Méliès*,[7] repeated so many of his earlier mistakes that it is virtually useless for the historian. *Georges Méliès* by Georges Sadoul[8] appeared in 1962, shortly after the centenary exhibition, the catalogue of which has some useful material, was held at the Musée des Arts Décoratifs, Paris, in 1961. Sadoul's book has its faults—there are many historical errors in it and the filmography is hastily compiled and muddled—but it is a comprehensive and important one. In 1963 Jacques Deslandes' extended essay, *Le Boulevard du Cinéma à l'époque de Georges Méliès*,[9] appeared. It established him as a faultlessly objective historian, a view reinforced by the appearance of the first two volumes of his *Histoire comparée du cinéma*, the second volume[10] of which, written in collaboration with Jacques Richard, is vital to any understanding of the first decade of the cinema. His exemplary scholarship has helped me greatly in the preparation of this book. Madeleine Malthête-Méliès published a pamphlet called *Georges Méliès, créateur du spectacle cinématographique*[11] in 1961, a prelude to the lengthy book about her grandfather which appeared in 1973.[12] More a banal romance than a biography, and full of mistakes, the 443 pages of this most recent work do contain some new information. The unreliability of so many of these previous sources is founded on their acceptance of the more diffuse writings of Georges Méliès himself, who towards the end of his life was asked to reminisce about the past. These reminiscences are not very trustworthy. He had never really come to terms with his demise as a film-maker, and he attempted to lay blame where he could, on his brother Gaston for instance. Showmanship and embellishment were his response to historians eager to fabricate a picaresque Méliès "myth". It is the aim of the present work to demystify that "myth" and thereby reveal Méliès' true genius.

Life and Work (1861–1938)

"At long last we would really witness gods ascending rainbows to their castles in the sky, horses galloping among the clouds, and sirens at the bottom of the ocean. And we would take it for real. Above all this is what I would ask of the cinema."—Claude Lévi-Strauss

Méliès' father was born in 1815 at Lavelanet, Ariège, a department at the foot of the Pyrenees. Jean-*Louis*-Stanislas Méliès was one of the sons of François Méliès, cloth-fuller, a craft that had been practised locally for two thousand years. Louis became a member of a masonic order that encouraged its candidates to travel around the country and practise their craft, so he took to the road as a journeyman boot and shoemaker, under the name of 'Carcassonne—L'Ami du Courage'. Seven years later, in 1843, he settled down in Paris upon marriage to a Dutch girl, Johannah-Catherine Schuering, one of the three daughters of the bootmaker to The Hague court. Born in 1819 at Schweningue, near The Hague, she and her family had moved to Paris after their factory had burned down. The couple met as hands in the same factory. Catherine helped Louis to educate himself. A couple of years passed before they were installed in their own workshop, where Louis exploited a new process for mechanically stitching the legs of boots. Sons Henri and Gaston were born in 1844 and 1852 respectively. In 1859 he opened a workshop in the Boulevard Saint-Martin, and in the years to follow factories at 36 Rue Meslay and 57 Rue Taylor. By the time Georges, the third son, was born, his father was well on the way to becoming a multi-millionaire (in francs) and the owner of substantial property, including tenement houses and a country villa. Marie-*Georges*-Jean Méliès was born on December 8 1861, at 29 Boulevard Saint-Martin, Paris.

Louis Méliès.

When he was seven Georges went to school at the Lycée Impérial at Vanves, near Paris. During the war of 1870 the school was bombarded by the Prussians, so the pupils were evacuated to Paris, and Georges became a boarder at the Lycée Louis-le-Grand, an institution Baudelaire had attended.

The dramatist Maurice Donnay, a contemporary of Georges Méliès, has painted a gloomy picture of this ancient and prestigious school, "this sombre prison", where life was conducted with "the mathematical punctuality of a barracks".[1] The pupils, in classes of forty, spent the day in tiled classrooms badly lit by grilled windows, under the watchful gaze of their teacher seated on a platform above their heads. For grammar and the humanities the school was reputed to be the best in Paris. To break the monotony of scholastic life there were frequent cold baths and occasional concerts at which the famous actors Coquelin aîné, Mounet-Sully and Mme Favart would recite sentimental and patriotic verses to an audience that included future academicians, politicians and police-chiefs.

On his own admission Georges Méliès was an average pupil, except in drawing, at which he excelled. His passion for sketching even got him into trouble for, as he said:

Méliès, the compulsive draughtsman.

he worked like the devil at drawing and, if there were good enough reports from his teachers, there were also many punishments for following this artistic passion at the wrong times. But it proved too strong for him, and while he should have been studying a French dissertation or Latin verse his pen was drawing portraits and caricatures of his teachers and school chums, or inventing some fantastic palace or an original landscape that already looked a bit like a theatre set. His exercise books, and even his text-books, were soon completely covered. This did not win the approval of his schoolmasters, and earned him countless lengthy detentions . . . As if there's any way to thwart vocation![2]

By the time he was ten Méliès was constructing Punch and Judy shows and cardboard sets, which "were to earn him quite a bit of stick as well".[3]

On July 20 1880, Georges Méliès received his baccalauréat. Before performing his military service he was given a job as a supervisor of accounts in his father's factory. On November 12 1881, he was conscripted as a second-class private into the 113th Infantry Regiment. He was promoted to private first-class (May 12 1882), and then corporal (November 12 1882), and was soon posted to Abbéville. On October 24 1883, he was transferred to the 45th Regiment of the Line and stationed at Laôn. He was demobilised sometime during 1884, and placed on reserve on November 7 1886.

During his military career Méliès spent some time at Blois, a town half-way between Tours and Orléans, where he must have visited the estate of the conjuror Jean-Eugène Robert-Houdin—whose theatre he had first seen as a boy in 1871, and was to buy later—a few miles away at Saint-Gervais. Robert-Houdin's estate, 'Le Prieuré', became the first electrically operated one in the world in 1857, when the magician installed such novelties as a burglar alarm, electric alarm clocks to wake his servants, an automatic feeding machine for his horse, and a device with which he could retard or advance all the clocks in his home as he pleased. For the further amusement of friends Robert-Houdin installed optical illusions in a pavilion in the grounds of his villa.

It has been claimed[4] that Méliès took painting lessons from Gustave Moreau during 1883. There are two good reasons why this is most unlikely: firstly, he was in the army at that time; and secondly, Moreau only began teaching in 1891, and there is no evidence to suggest that he gave private lessons before that date.

On leaving the army Méliès went to London, where he stayed with a friend of his father's, the proprietor of an emporium selling ready-made clothes, who took him on as an employee. Because he spoke and understood little English at this time and sought a recreation where language wasn't a barrier, he began to frequent the Egyptian Hall in Piccadilly, which was a magic theatre run by John Nevil Maskelyne and George Alfred Cooke. There he saw spec-

The Egyptian Hall, after 1896. Note the sign for 'Improved Animated Photographs'. Nevil Maskelyne's camera/projector, the *Mutagraph*, was patented on May 28 1896.

tacular illusions like *The Floating Lady, The Tell Tale Hat, Zach the Hermit* (which had a winking moon, automatic talking parrot, mechanical snake, animated walking stick and levitated hero) and *The Light and Dark Séance* (which ended with an illuminated skeleton whose jaws rattled and whose head left his trunk and floated above the audience). An extravaganza called *Sennacherib in Two Parts and Screvins in Two Pieces* must have deeply impressed Méliès for his own stage spectacle, *American Spiritualistic Mediums, or the Recalcitrant Decapitated Man*, presented twelve years after the first production of Maskelyne and Cooke's entertainment in 1879, bears a striking resemblance to it.

J. N. Maskelyne spinning plates.

Maskelyne made a name for himself by publicly denouncing the deceptions of the Davenport Brothers. Self-styled spirit mediums, the Davenports, once tied and housed inside a cabinet, caused tambourines and guitars to float through the darkened auditorium—supposedly manifestations of a spirit world—and climaxed their performance with themselves appearing to float up to the ceiling. What really happened was that when the lights went down the medium untied himself, drew a telescopic rod from his clothing, fixed to the end of it tambourines and inflated gloves, coated in phosphorous so they glowed, and then dangled these objects over the heads of the audience. When called upon to become airborne himself a lay-figure was substituted for the medium at the last moment and hauled on high by wires and pulleys. Maskelyne used similar devices himself: it was the bogus 'spiritualism' of the Americans that he disliked. Like his English mentor, Méliès satirised the Davenports in a 1902 film, *The Cabinet Trick of the Davenport Brothers.*

On show at the Egyptian Hall, 'England's Home of Mystery', were four automata, essential items in any self-respecting magician's repertoire: *Psycho*, the Hindu whist-player *Zoe*, who drew portraits of Darwin and Disraeli, *Fanfare*, the cornet-player, and *Labial*, who played the euphonium. The Egyptian Hall was to become one of the first British theatres to show films in 1896. For a time David Devant, a conjuror who appeared regularly with Maskelyne after 1893* was Méliès' sole agent for the sale of films and cameras in the U.K. Devant was to appear in a number of pioneering films, for R. W. Paul (1896), Méliès (1897), and

The Cabinet Trick of the Davenport Brothers (1902). The man in the black overcoat is Méliès.

Mutoscope and Biograph (1903).

When he returned to Paris, Méliès was intent on entering the École des Beaux-Arts and becoming a painter. His father, however, would not hear of it—nearly half a century and widely differing sensibilities separated the two men—and Georges, not without ill-feeling, was obliged to take his place with his brothers, who had both suffered the same loss of liberty, Henri in 1873, Gaston in 1878, in the family business. Georges became overseer of the factory machinery, a position which enlarged his knowledge of mechanics. This was to prove useful later on.

Meanwhile Méliès was learning how to conjure, taking lessons from Émile Voisin, who ran a conjuring shop in the Rue Vieille-du-Temple. Soon he began to give perform-ances, first of all in the salons of family friends, then at the

* It is impossible, therefore, that Méliès could have seen him perform there in 1884, as several historians suggest.

Méliès' drawing of a scene from *The Lilliputian Minuet* (1905), includes a self-portrait of the conjuror.

Galérie Vivienne, a small theatre given over to puppet shows and comic-opera. He worked, too, at developing the art of the monologue, a form that was much in vogue thanks to the actors Félix Galipaux and Coquelin cadet. "This," said Méliès in his memoirs, "is how he became acquainted with the métier of actor and comedian." When performing Méliès dressed in a red jacket with gold buttons, knee breeches and silk stockings.

On June 29 1885, Georges Méliès married Eugénie Génin, a young Dutch girl, the illegitimate daughter of a close friend of Georges' uncle, who presented him with a substantial dowry, provided by her guardians, Mme Coussy and M. and Mme Mourguye. It had been hoped that he would marry the sister of his brothers' wives, who were sisters. The newlyweds settled on the fifth floor of 5 Rue Taylor. Throughout her life Eugénie was to remain a timid, placid person, somewhat of an outsider where her husband's family and professional activities were concerned. In his father's factory down the street from their apartment Méliès set up a workshop where, over a period of three years, he reconstructed some of Robert-Houdin's automata with the help of Eugène Calmels, the house-mechanic and later projectionist at the Théâtre Robert-Houdin.

In 1888 Louis Méliès retired and ceded the direction of his factories to his sons, thereby providing Georges, who sold his share to his brothers, with enough money to buy the Théâtre Robert-Houdin from the widow of Émile Robert-Houdin, the son of the famous conjuror. On July 1 1888, he became its director. With his wife and daughter Georgette, born in February, he moved into an apartment close by at 22 Rue Chauchat.

Jean-Eugène Robert-Houdin (1805–71) had reformed conjuring by dispensing with the draped tables, gaudy apparatus and ostentatious costumes of his predecessors and replacing them with simple, well-designed pieces of apparatus and the conventional clothes of a bourgeois dressed for dinner. His presentation was unflagging, genial and witty. His tricks included *The Ethereal Suspension,* in which a boy was suspended in mid-air, *The Fantastic Orange Tree,* which bore fruit under mysterious circumstances, and *Robert-Houdin's Portfolio,* from which he produced doves, bonnets, saucepans and his son.

Robert-Houdin, assisted by his son Émile, presents *The Fantastic Orange Tree,* c. 1845.

If Robert-Houdin's illusions were completely convincing, they were also extremely simple. He made use of sleight-of-hand, substitutions and feints, as well as a hidden shelf under his table to hide objects. In *The Surprising Silk Handkerchief,* for example, he drew pre-concealed feathers from his sleeve. With *The Inexhaustible Bottle* Robert-Houdin could fill numerous glasses because many of them were already full of colourless fluid. The bottle was pneumatically controlled and 'played' like a woodwind instrument, 'stops' being released to provide liquor. In *Marvellous Fishing* he produced a bowl of fish from a secret pocket in his coat-tails. During his act Robert-Houdin showed a number of mechanical figures he had constructed himself: *Antonio Davolio, the Trapezist, The Pastry-Cook of the Palais-Royal* and *Sophos, the Domino Player.* None of these were true automata however, as they depended upon the help of an invisible assistant, either in the wings or inside the mechanism, or the invisible assistance of electricity or compressed air, to make them work.

Robert-Houdin's automaton, *Antonio Davolio, the Trapezist.*

In terms of influence it was Maskelyne rather than Robert-Houdin who affected Méliès. The generation separating the French and English showmen had seen Maskelyne develop the use of dramatic narratives to connect and enhance the

Exterior of the Théâtre
Robert-Houdin.

tricks performed piecemeal by Robert-Houdin. J. N.
Maskelyne's son, Nevil, wrote:

> Since the principles of magical procedure are inadequate
> to provide the conditions requisite for dramatic effect, we
> are bound to fall back on the principles of drama for the
> main outlines of our presentation . . . The magical items
> are, as it were, beads held together and supported by the
> thread of dramatic interest. Thus connected, the beads
> form a chain of harmonious proportions.[5]

The combining of magic and drama was Maskelyne's
great contribution.

The Théâtre Robert-Houdin, founded in 1843 at the

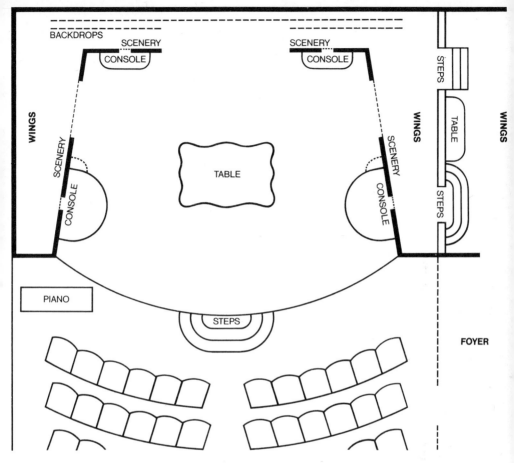

Palais-Royal, moved to 8 Boulevard des Italiens in 1852, where it occupied a small room on the first floor with about 200 seats. Originally papered in red and gold, after its restoration in 1901 the stage represented a simple white and gold drawing-room of the Louis XV period. Georges Méliès described the theatre thus:

Organisation of the stage at the Robert-Houdin.

> Robert-Houdin had planned and equipped his theatre with extreme care, solely for prestidigitation. The resulting amenities were superb and facilitated any trick that depended on more than sleight-of-hand. If the facilities are not at hand for marvels that involve dexterity, mechanics, electricity, levers, pulleys, trapdoors, and the help of an invisible assistant, then these splendid wonders cannot be. For this reason some fine illusions and tricks were to be seen only at the Robert-Houdin.[6]

Furthermore, Robert-Houdin had taken the precaution of

installing his own automatic 'chef de claque', a pair of shells which, when activated by an electrical impulse controlled by the conjuror, struck each other loudly, thereby stimulating the audience to applause.

Under its new management the Théâtre Robert-Houdin, which Méliès had refurbished and probably hoped would compete, on a small scale at least, with the Châtelet, a popular and grandiose Parisian theatre devoted to the production of adventure stories and pantomimes like *Robinson Crusoe*, *Around the World in Eighty Days* and *Cinderella*, reopened in October 1888 to virtually empty houses. On October 17, Duperrey, a long-standing artiste at the theatre, went to the new proprietor's office and drew Méliès' attention to the deplorable state of affairs. At 8.25 that evening there were only four spectators in the theatre; by curtain-up there were sixteen; by the end of the show twenty-eight. The tricks were old. It was to be ten years before the Robert-Houdin began to show a profit, and only after the inception of animated photographs.

From 1888 to 1907 Méliès invented thirty or so 'theatrical compositions', many of them variations of older illusions (Maskelyne's), a number of which were put on the market by his friend, the theatrical supplier Voisin, who had helped him make a start in conjuring. In this way Méliès' illusions were seen in fairgrounds and music-halls long before his films were shown there. At the Théâtre Robert-Houdin many famous artistes performed in his (and their own) productions: Buatier de Kolta, the dwarf la Fée Mab, Okita, Duperrey, Raynaly, Arnould, Folletto, Harmington, Legris and Carmelli appeared there, as did Jehanne d'Alcy, who was to become Méliès' mistress and, in 1925, the second Mme Méliès. Piano accompaniment was provided by M. or Mme Leclerc, M. or Mme Rehm and Mme Caroline Chélu, and Jules David, alias Marius, helped on stage. Georges Méliès rarely performed.

Most of Méliès' stage spectaculars* were conceived during the period 1888–97. *The Fairy of the Flowers*, for example, was an optical illusion based on a pun, 'un parterre', which means both 'audience' and 'flower-bed', and is the trick's common denominator. An inclined sheet of glass and clever lighting enabled the spectators to see themselves as in a mirror. Their image was then transformed, by a shift in the lighting, into a bed of flowers in the centre of which was

---

* A list of these will be found in the trickography at the back of the book.

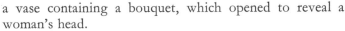

a vase containing a bouquet, which opened to reveal a woman's head.

In *Hypnotism, Catalepsy, Magnetism,* also known as *Catalepsy and the Cops,*

Monsieur Harmington, a disciple of Mesmer, asks for and finds a subject in the room when a young artiste called Marius steps forward. M. Harmington makes him execute all sorts of follies. After various passes smartly executed by the hypnotist, M. Marius suddenly becomes as stiff as a board and, spinning on his heels, falls forward. If M. Harmington hadn't rushed to his aid he would certainly have cracked his head on the floor . . . He lifts and places him as he would a plank across two suitably spaced chairs. M. Jules David (Marius) remains immobile. To crown the audience's amazement M. Harmington seats himself triumphantly on Marius' abdomen. At that moment, as Marius' extraordinary exercise comes to an end, a gendarme rushes on to the stage in an attempt to implement the recent regulations concerning hypnotism. But he is himself subjugated by Monsieur Harmington and laid low by the mesmeriser. As the curtain falls the representative of authority is struggling against the catalepsy that is overtaking him.[7]

Drawing by Méliès of *The Yellow Dwarf* (1890).

The conjuror Legris levitates a table in *Spirit Phenomena,* a stage spectacular presented in 1907.

American Spiritualistic Mediums, or the Recalcitrant Decapitated Man concerns the adventures of Professor Barbenfouillis (literally 'whiskers-in-a-tangle'), whose head is cut off by a conjuror because he won't stop talking about spiritualism. The head is shut in a box where it continues its discourse. When no one is looking the professor's body grabs its head and runs off, the conjuror and his assistant giving chase. Just

LE DÉCAPITÉ RÉCALCITRANT
Bouffonnerie Fantastique

au Théâtre ROBERT-HOUDIN

A gauche, M. BRUNEVAL *(Rôle du • préparateur • DUBOCAL).* – Au milieu, l'Illusionniste LEGRIS.

A droite, M. Georges MÉLIÈS *(Rôle du • professeur • BARBENFOUILLIS.*

A scene from *American Spiritualistic Mediums, or the Recalcitrant Decapitated Man* (1891), with *dramatis personæ.*

then, through a window, a skeleton carrying Barbenfouillis' head is seen to zoom by at top speed, followed by the decapitated man's body bounding after his head, the artiste and the servant in pursuit of both. Barbenfouillis returns on the scene, but instead of his own the headless man has mistakenly grabbed the skeleton's skull and put it on his shoulders. The servant is seen to look for the real head, which is locked in a piece of gothic furniture in the centre of the stage. The professor has been placed in a sarcophagus. A gun goes off. Instantly the head shut in the furniture replaces the skull on the shoulder of the professor who, while astonished to rediscover his head back on, continues with his discourse. Finally, to shut him up he is suspended from the ceiling. The curtain slowly descends. Barbenfouillis though is still chattering away to the audience:

Compare this poster for
Maskelyne's extrava-
ganza, *Sennacherib in Two
Parts and Screvins in Two
Pieces*, with Méliès'
'bouffonerie fantastique'.

'Ladies and gentlemen, I hold you all as witnesses to the
crime that has just been perpetrated!' (Howling) 'I'm
dying . . . a victim of my devotion to science!' (Lowering
his voice more and more, like a dying man) 'But before
departing for the other world, permit me to tell you,'
(shouting with all his might), 'that since the time of the
Greeks, the era of the Romans . . .'

'Oh no! Curtain! Curtain!' cries the conjuror, and the
curtain falls amidst the spectators' roars of laughter.[8]

The action of *The Enchanted Spring*

takes place in the reign of Louis XV, in a grove in the
park of Versailles through the middle of which flows a
spring to which legend attributes a magical power. After
a young marquis has been imprudent enough to drink at
this bewitched source a demon appears and, to punish the
nobleman, condemns his fiancée to lose her head. The
latter will remain imprisoned in the spring. In fact the
marquis sees the detached head of his intended floating in
space in the middle of a confluence of light. He tries to get
his hands on it, but she is transformed into a dove.[9]

The passionate rhetoric of *An Up-to-Date Mountebank*, a
"tremendous comico-spiritual production by G. Méliès", is
reason enough for noting the

incredible adventures of Sir John Patt de Cok coming to
rest his spleen at the sanatorium of the Illustrioussimo
Giuseppe Barbenmacaroni, well supplied with banknotes
and undergoing the excruciating treatments of this raving
fin-de-siècle mountebank, until the final trick explosion of

A chromatrope lantern slide.

the phlegmatic son of Albion who, having swallowed a dynamite pill, explodes into a thousand bits, and whose head, still alive, is encased in the dial of a clock where it chants the final tirade in this astounding fairy story.[10]

The performances at the Théâtre Robert-Houdin ended with the showing of lantern slides. Photographic views of different lands, lever slides (mechanised plates sliding horizontally to give the illusion of boats on a river, falling snow, etc.), chromatropes (consisting of two decorated glass discs turning in opposite directions to produce cyclic patterns) and a series of comic images called *The Burlesque Waxworks*, hand-painted by Méliès, with a mordant commentary from E. Raynaly, were projected. "The projections were by lime-light using a number of Molteni lanterns placed in such a way as to allow the tableaux to dissolve into each other. The system was analogous to the dissolve in film-making."[11] In 1890 *Chinese Shadows* (silhouettes)—*The Surgeon, The Barber, Brutal Explosion* and *A Comfortable Inn*—were included as well.

After *The Golden Cage* (1897) Méliès devoted himself to making films. The fact that he recommenced the presentation of illusions at the Robert-Houdin in 1904 is revealing: this date undoubtedly marks a flagging in his cinematic activities. In the period between 1905 and 1907 he produced four new spectaculars. Méliès used film to record and enhance these theatrical productions.

From August 1889 until February 1890 Méliès contributed political caricatures, under the anagrammatical pseudonym of 'Geo. Smile' and under the influence of André Gill, to twenty-six numbers of *La Griffe (The Talon)*, a satirical journal edited by his cousin Adolphe Méliès, an attorney. *La Griffe* was the sworn enemy of General Boulanger, who planned to overthrow the Republic and put the Royalist pretender, the Comte de Paris, in power. Méliès claimed that if this had come about he "would have risked exile, at the very least, for he had dedicated to the 'brav' général', as the popular singer Paulus called him, a number of biting caricatures ridiculing this would-be Caesar."[12] When Méliès came to film Paulus singing several hymns to Boulanger in 1897 he omitted their titles from his catalogue.

It is necessary, however, to keep Geo. Smile's 'subversive' activities in perspective, for they have been greatly exaggerated. Méliès was no anarchist. During the 1880s and into the 1890s anarchism was viewed sympathetically by the

LA GRIFFE

DIRECTEUR-RÉDACTEUR EN CHEF : ADOLPHE MÉLIÈS

RÉDACTION ET ADMINISTRATION : 9, PLACE DES VOSGES, 9.

TROP DE PRESSION !!! par GÉO. SMILE

A caricature of Boulanger by 'Geo. Smile' on the cover of *La Griffe*. The first of numerous exploding characters, cf. *The Man With the Rubber Head* (1902).

working class and a section of the bourgeoisie as well. The terrorist acts of Ravachol, Vaillant and Émile Henry served to unsettle the political smugness of the Third Republic, a complacency which could just as well bring reactionaries like Boulanger to the fore too. Anti-clericalism, which led to the separation of Church and State in 1906, was commonplace.

It seems that Méliès was nothing more than a staunch republican, as the second Mme Méliès said: "Méliès was pro-Dreyfus and anti-Boulanger. Anti-clerical? Oh, not really! He was a free-thinker. He didn't care."[13]

Lumière's *Cinématographe.*

R. W. Paul's *Animatographe.*

The *kinétograph* (right).

On December 28 1895, Georges Méliès was one of those invited to the first public showing of the Lumière *Cinématographe* at the Grand Café, an exhibition compèred by the inventor's father Antoine Lumière, a photographer who, incidentally, had shortly before rented a studio above the Théâtre Robert-Houdin. Like the Isola brothers Méliès tried to buy the new invention and was turned down. The machine came on the market in late 1897. Meanwhile he looked elsewhere.

In February 1896 he travelled to London to buy a projector from R. W. Paul, an instrument maker who manufactured counterfeit *Kinetoscopes*. By studying this mechanism, the *Animatographe*, Méliès was able to design a camera, the construction of which he left to a mechanic called Lucien Korsten. There is some confusion on this point. It seems possible that Méliès simply acquired the rights to a machine developed by his friends the Isola brothers, called the *Isolatograph*. Nevertheless, in March Méliès had a camera-projector which he baptised the *Kinétograph* and nicknamed "my machine-gun". That same month he went to London again and bought a crate of Kodak film. Upon his return to Paris he discovered that the film was not perforated. A clumsy machine for this purpose, which punched two holes at a time, was made for him by a man called Lapipe.

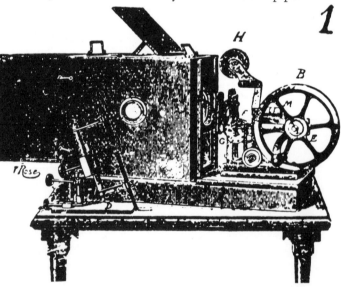

On April 4 1896, Méliès presented his first film show at the Théâtre Robert-Houdin. Edison's *Kinetoscope* films, boxing kangaroos, serpentine dancers, seascapes, white

silhouettes on black, were on the bill. During May and June
he took his first films in the garden of his house at Montreuil,
near Paris. *Playing Cards, Conjuring* and *Gardener Burning
Weeds*, snapshots filmed à la Lumière, had the magician's
family, servants and friends as actors. *Watering Flowers* was
a comedy, a pastiche of Louis Lumière's *L'Arroseur arrosé* (*A
Joke on the Gardener*). July 13 saw the annual closure of the
theatre. Méliès went to Le Havre and Trouville for his holidays, where he filmed a *Panorama of Havre Taken From a Boat,
Arrival of a Train* (*Joinville Station*) and *The Beach at Villiers
in a Gale*. The latter film conveniently gives us an oppor-
tunity to measure Méliès' veracity. In his memoirs he
describes how, because the magazine of his camera could
hold only 20 metres of film at a time, on this occasion he
was forced to dismantle the apparatus between takes and
cart the whole lot to a photographer's house nearby where
he recharged it:

What gymnastics! He was alone and dared not leave anything behind in case it was interfered with, and yet . . . to
cart it back and forth! You can imagine how tired one
becomes of repeating the same operation twenty times
a day. And there were several kilometres to be covered
across beaches where one sank up to the knees in the soft
sand. But Méliès was filled with sacred fire.[14]

Even if Méliès had made more than one take, it is impossible
to swallow the idea of twenty! This vivid paragraph is
typical of the memoirs, a document that has long served as
the definitive guide to his life and work.

Méliès' first films are close to Lumière's earliest efforts. So
the Lumière/Méliès polarity, hitherto a convenience for historians too shortsighted to look further than monolithic
categories like 'realism' and 'fantasy', is really nothing but a
red herring. For both Lumière and Méliès at this time it was
almost a reflex action to take snapshots, for they were confined within the impressionistic aesthetic of the everyday
photographer; indeed, one of Lumière's first films was of a
group of amateur photographers on an outing, *Landing of
Members of the Congress* (1895). Lumière, who was more
interested in his other technical researches, made few films
himself, preferring to train other men, like Promio, Mesguish, Doublier and Perrigot, to do it for him. Méliès' first
films are like Lumière's because in these brief first months
he was uncertain of the potential of the new medium and

looked for guidance. Although Lumière made the occasional trick film—thereby confusing the issue still further—he never went beyond the snapshot stage; Méliès did. Given the disparity in their contribution to the cinema, what really separates Lumière and Méliès are two disciplines of *still* photography, one illustrative and impressionistic, the other spectacular and full of tricks. We might call on two hypothetical images to underline this difference. In the first, a bourgeois poses stiffly for his portrait, his eyes fixed on some distant horizon; in the second, the same man poses in the same manner, except that a ghost looks over his shoulder: one image calls the other into question.

On August 1 the theatre reopened. Films and cameras were on sale in a room at 14 Passage de l'Opéra, and could be demonstrated at the Robert-Houdin from 2–6 pm, or at the evening show. On September 2, Korsten, Méliès and Lucien Reulos, an associate to whom he had been introduced by Leborgne, an old friend from his army days, took out a patent, no. 259.444 (British patent no. 19,446), on the *Kinétograph*, which was to receive a gold medal at that year's Exposition de Travail. On December 20 the Star Film trademark, a star containing the initials 'M' (for Méliès) and 'R' (for Reulos) appeared for the first time. A motto was coined, "The Whole World Within Reach", and it was.

During 1896 Méliès produced seventy-eight films, seventy-seven of which were 65 feet in length, the capacity of a spool. Méliès, Reulos, and Leclerc were the cameramen. *The Vanishing Lady* was inspired by one of Buatier de Kolta's illusions. To make his seated lady disappear Méliès simply stopped the camera, allowed her to quit the scene, and recommenced filming, before taking the trick a stage further. A skeleton appeared on the seat and was covered with a sheet. When this was removed the lady (Jehanne d'Alcy) had reappeared in its place. This was Méliès' first substitution trick. The last film of 1896, *The Devil's Castle*, was 195 feet long, that is three lengths of film spliced together. Lasting just over three minutes, it was Méliès' first big production, and the first vampire film ever made:

The picture shows a room in a mediaeval castle; carved stone pillars, low doors and vaulted ceiling. A huge bat flies in and circles around. It is suddenly transformed into Mephistopheles. He walks around, makes a magic pass, and a large cauldron appears and out of it, in a great cloud of smoke, there emerges a beautiful lady. At another

Three images from *The Vanishing Lady* (1896).

magic pass, a little old man comes out of the floor carrying a big book. Then the cauldron disappears. And so it goes on. Cavaliers, ghosts, a skeleton and witches appear and disappear at a sign from the Evil One. Finally one of the cavaliers produces a cross, and Mephistopheles throws up his hands and disappears in a cloud of smoke.[15]

To develop a film Méliès rolled it around a large glass bottle, stuck the two ends with wax and put it into a pail of the appropriate chemical. Later he constructed semicircular horizontal tanks with cranked wooden drums that turned inside them. Michaut was put in charge of developing. To make prints, negative and fresh positive film were run through the camera together, the whole exposed to a constant light source. Due to the vagaries of the sunlight which illuminated his productions the negatives varied in density. To overcome these irregularities the printing time was gauged proportionately, and the operator hand-cranked the camera at various speeds: "The sight of these machinists, sometimes cranking quickly, sometimes very slowly, without apparent reason, surprised the occasional visitor to the laboratories. Some must have asked themselves if the operator was not a little mad."[16] Later Méliès acquired printing and perforating machines from the firm of André Debrie.

Since location shooting in all weathers was impractical, Méliès decided to build a studio in the garden of his Montreuil home, at the intersection of 74bis Boulevard de l'Hôtel de Ville and 1–3 Rue François Debergue. This took from the end of September 1896 to March 1897. It was not the first film studio in the world (Edison's 'Black Maria' preceded it) but it was a significant and practical solution to the problem of wind, rain and primitive equipment, and it marked the interiorisation of his thought, a looking inward, a drawing up of creative energies for the years of intensive work ahead.

The studio was made of glass and looked like a big greenhouse. Méliès had designed it with a mind to the amount of space required to film a tableau 20 feet wide: the studio needed to be 55 feet long, 20 feet wide, and the apex of the roof 20 feet from the ground. At first the framework was constructed from wood, but this proved too weak to support the spars and glass of the roofing, so the wooden beams were strengthened or replaced by iron struts. The frosted glass roof was replaced by panes of clear glass just above the stage, on which the sun shone from 11 am to 3 pm. The stage itself was fitted with theatrical machinery such as trapdoors, winches and levers, and the studio was the same size as the Théâtre Robert-Houdin. There was no element of chance in this: Méliès was transposing his theatre to the film studio.

The design of the Montreuil studio was modified, when wings and balconies were added. Soon it was 42 feet wide and was backed by dressing rooms. A large hangar, the same size and fitted with canvas blinds, to keep it cool in summer, was constructed next to the studio for the use of the carpenters and scenery painters. The camera was moved back into a small shed, allowing tableaux 36 feet wide to be shot. Over the years buildings multiplied around the studio: a materials store, carpentry workshop and a wardrobe store containing hundreds of costumes, in the charge of Émile Gagean, appeared. Laboratories were installed too; this

The studio at Montreuil-sous-Bois, *c.* 1900. The lean-to at the left housed the camera. The slightly-unfurled canvas blinds fitted to the framework of the adjacent hangar can be seen on the right.

Preparing costumes for Star Film productions.

The studio's dressing-room.

saved time and meant that scenes could be reshot if necessary while the cast and sets were still assembled.

Films were shown at the Robert-Houdin until July 1 1897, when the theatre closed. It reopened on September 4 with evening performances devoted exclusively to films, which were projected with piano accompaniment, sound-effects from the wings and a spoken commentary. On holidays, Thursday and Sunday evenings and every afternoon conjuring was on the bill. All shows lasted two hours. During the Christmas holidays the pantomime *Cinderella*, performed by the Troupe Raymond, was presented as a supplementary matinée. In autumn Méliès and Reulos parted company, thus ending an alliance which had produced films, cameras and albums of photographs for sale. They had also marketed a small movie-camera for amateurs, the *Mirographe* (patented by de Goudeau and Leclerc, the cameraman/pianist), which

The *Mirographe*, inside and out.

sold badly. Their *Kinétograph* had been forced out of the market too, by the appearance of the *Cinématographe*. Méliès himself was to stick to cameras made by Gaumont, Demenÿ, Lumière and Pathé.

In 1897, he used electric arc-lights (an innovation) to film the singer Paulus performing a number of songs on the stage of the Robert-Houdin. Phonograph recordings* and films would be presented in synchronisation. *D. Devant, Conjuror* showed the English illusionist doing a turn. The Devil appeared on two more occasions, in *The Laboratory of Mephistopheles*, where "everything is so weird and fantastic that such a small trifle as a man turning into a donkey excites but passing notice",[17] and in *The Haunted Castle*, a film based on a stage spectacle produced in 1890. *After the Ball* is a stag film: Jehanne d'Alcy is bathed in soot (or dyed sand) by Jeanne Brady, a singer from the café-concert. The year's final

The scenery store.

* The British Institute of Recorded Sound has an unidentified Paulus recording in its collection.

film, *Faust and Marguerite*, was Méliès' first screen adaptation of a literary work.

The major innovation of 1897, however, was the 'reconstructed newsreel' (l'actualité reconstituée). Méliès had taken local newsreel film in September 1896 (*The Czar and his Cortège Going to Versailles*), but events taking place farther afield posed a problem. Lumière sent his cameramen all over the world to take newsreel and documentary film. Méliès decided to re-enact news stories in his studio. In this way he filmed the first reconstructed newsreels, scenes from the Greco-Turkish War of 1897, *War Episodes, Massacre in Crete* and *Sea Fighting in Greece*, for which models were used. *The Last Cartridges*, depicting an incident in the Franco–Prussian War of 1870 (hardly hot news!), was based upon a painting by Alfred de Neuville. It was then common practice to approximate the news: newspapers were unable to print photographs satisfactorily and engravings took their place. The news was also disseminated in the form of picture postcards and in the tableaux at wax museums like the Musée Grévin, "a kind of plastic newspaper in 3-dimensions, a newsreel in flesh and bone".[18]

Méliès supposedly discovered the substitution trick, which permits one object to change instantaneously into another, because his camera jammed as he was filming *The Place de l'Opéra* in 1896. (In which of the two films made at that location during the year it is not known, and, to confuse things still further, there is a third view of the Place de l'Opéra, shot at the beginning of 1898.) When the film in question was screened it could be seen that the break in shooting (while the jammed film was freed) had caused an omnibus to change into a hearse. This happy accident may have given Méliès the idea of using the substitution trick to change a skeleton into a living woman in *The Vanishing Lady* (1896). Assuming the incident did take place (and it could easily be picturesque window-dressing), was Méliès bowled over by its implications? Certainly not, for between the chance discovery and its subsequent utilisation in *The Vanishing Lady* Méliès found the time to film *fifty* more actualities. Let us not forget that in making this film Méliès wanted to simulate an illusion performed by the conjuror Buatier de Kolta and that Edison had already used a cinematic substitution—though not in the metaphoric way that Méliès employed it—in his *Mary Queen of Scots* (1895), a film the Frenchman must have known. The Place de l'Opéra incident, if it occurred at all, may have underlined the metaphorical possibilities of the substitution trick. There is a distinction to be made between substituting an object for a counterfeit representation of itself (a dummy replacing Queen Mary on the scaffold) and changing one object into another quite different one. It is the difference between tautology and metaphor.

On February 3 1898, Louis Méliès died, and the theatre was closed until May 1. Méliès had installed laboratories in the Passage de l'Opéra, had engaged Lallement as a printer, and was selling films to fairs in France and music-halls in England. His day was a full one. He got up at 6 am and was at the studio by 7, building scenery, accessories and making

Méliès, at right, helps with the props. An employee with mallet and chisel labours on the omnibus that will appear in *Off to Bloomingdale Asylum* (1901).

repairs until 5 in the evening. After dressing hurriedly he left for Paris, arriving at 6 o'clock. The hour between 6 and 7 was spent in his office. After dinner he was at the theatre by 8 pm, seeing that all went well and sketching ideas during the show. Afterwards he returned to Montreuil, finally getting to bed around midnight. Fridays and Saturdays were reserved for the filming of tableaux prepared during the week.

Following the practice of the day Méliès began to project advertising films on to an open-air screen on the Boulevard des Italiens. His little daughter Georgette was the projectionist. Méliès made publicity shorts to sell hats, mustard, flour, corsets, hair-restorer, shoe-polish, beer, whiskey, chocolate and tortoiseshell combs. In the film for *Delion Hats*, rabbits passed into a machine only to appear as hats, which became rabbits again by running the film backwards. In *Dewar's Whiskey*, family portraits descended from their frames to sample the drink. Méliès sprouted abundant hair on his hands as well as his head after using *Xour Lotion* for baldness: "I looked horrible, a real orang-utan. Everybody laughed".[19]

In 1898 Méliès produced several ingenious reconstructed newsreels of scenes of American intervention in Cuba and the Philippines (April–August), notably *A View of the Wreck of the 'Maine'* and *Divers At Work on the Wreck of the 'Maine'*. A painted backcloth representing the sunken battleship was shot through a gauze curtain with seaweed painted on it and a large aquarium, containing real fish and water agitated by a screw, was set five feet from the camera. In *The Temptation of Saint Anthony* the holy man was hard pressed to prevent himself being seduced by the phantasms of his own imagination, in the form of pretty girls in flimsy costumes. *The Astronomer's Dream, or The Man In the Moon*, predicting the famous *A Trip to the Moon* (1902), was a cinematic version of *The Moon's Pranks, or the Misadventures of Nostradamus*, performed on the stage of the Robert-Houdin in July 1891.

Georges Sadoul was exaggerating when he claimed that the appearance of Albert Allis Hopkins' book, *Magic, Stage Illusions and Scientific Diversions, Including Trick Photography*, published in New York and London in autumn 1897, was enough to transform Méliès' aesthetic. Méliès was already familiar with trick photography, since it was common knowledge by this time. Hopkins' book undoubtedly provided a convenient resumé of contemporary photographic trickery, for Sadoul in 1961 if not for Méliès in 1897. It describes the techniques of photography on a black ground, spirit photography and duplex photography.

Photography on a black ground allowed the production of composite and often amusing images by manipulation close to the camera lens of a blackened piece of cardboard, provided with an aperture corresponding to the place preserved in the definitive picture for the object one wished to isolate. Complementary exposures were needed to assemble these photographs, and the subjects were shot for emphasis before a black background, usually in the shape of a doorway.

Spirit photography, known since the 1860s, meant photographing a shrouded 'spirit' against a black background and then superimposing the image or scene that the spirit is supposed to inhabit.

Duplex photography involved the use of a special frame with two shutters, operating like the leaves of a door, mounted in front of the camera lens. One leaf stayed shut

'Man in a Bottle', from
Hopkins, p. 431. Photo-
graphy on a black ground.

'Spirit Picture', from
Hopkins, p. 435.

'Illustration of Duplex
Photography', from
Hopkins, p. 443.

while half of the negative was exposed. The process was
repeated, with the result that the same person would appear
twice on one print.

Méliès realised that these techniques, which are closely
related to the optical trickery used in the magic theatre,
could be adapted to cinematography. Using spirit photography he filmed *The Triple Lady* and *The Cave of the Demons*,
in which the rocky walls of a cavern could be seen through
the transparent bodies of a number of ghosts. Using a variation of photography on a black ground and the duplex
method he made *The Four Troublesome Heads*, in which a
magician removes his head three times over, a film that predicts the celebrated *Melomaniac* of 1903. From this point on,
a doorway or large fireplace always delineates the black area
within which something will appear.

These techniques were particularly suited to satisfy Méliès'
appetite for the phantasmagoric. It was the perfection of new
magic-lantern techniques a century earlier that had led to the
surfacing of the phantasmagoric tradition. Robertson
(Étienne Gaspar Robert) had presented his *Fantasmagorie* in
Paris in 1794. Using a movable lantern Robertson projected
painted slides on to a triple layer of gauze curtain. Robertson's imagery related to Gothic fiction, with its storms,
spectacular scenery, ruined castles, gloomy chapels, secret
passages, cryptic messages, visionary heroines and, of course,
ghosts. David Devant gives a graphic description of
Robertson's entertainment:

After spending nearly ten years of work on his apparatus,
Robertson opened his ghost show in Paris in 1794. It was
principally worked by a movable projecting lantern and

Robertson's *Fantasma-gorie.*

awesome figures painted on glass slides projected on to a screen, also on to clouds of smoke emerging from braziers. This entertainment was given at the Pavillon de l'Exchequer. It was a great success, and later moved to a disused chapel. This was approached by corridors of tombs and other monuments, which helped produce the weird atmosphere necessary. The interior of the chapel was draped in black, and the only light came from a single lamp burning with a pale flame.

Robertson came forward and gave a sort of lecture on sorcerers, claimed that he was no charlatan, but could raise the dead. He asked the audience the names of their dead relatives and produced apparitions of them; during this the single lamp went out, while a storm with thunder and lightning took place and a church bell solemnly tolled, music was heard and a ghost appeared. This weird performance of Robertson's was given for six years with an enormous success in Paris and other large cities.[20]

In his memoirs Robertson lists his phantasmagoric repertoire.[21] Among the thirty subjects are *The Temptation of Saint Anthony, The Three Graces Changed Into Skeletons, The Fairies' Dance, Venus Cajoling a Hermit* and *The Bleeding Nun*: just the subjects—with their optical trickery and gallows humour—that Méliès was to bring to cinematography.

The phantasmagoric tradition was recharged when Henry Dircks, a civil engineer, and John Henry Pepper, a professor at London's Royal Polytechnic Institution, showed *Pepper's Ghost* in 1862. A popular variation of the illusion showed a man in a coffin 'dissolving' into a skeleton in a coffin. Lamps illuminating the living man were turned down at the same

'An X-Ray Illusion Upon
the Stage', a variation of
Pepper's Ghost.

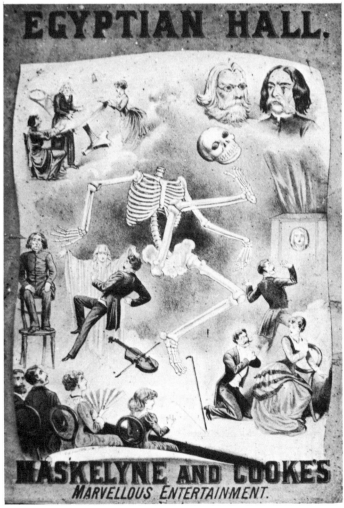

Poster for *A Spirit Case or
Mrs. Daffodil Downey's
Light and Dark Séance*.

time as lamps illuminating the skeleton were turned up. An intermediate sheet of glass, set at 45° to both coffins, provided the 'screen' for this transformation. The skeleton was, of course, concealed from the audience at all times.

J. N. Maskelyne contributed to the tradition. In *A Spirit Case or Mrs. Daffodil Downy's Light and Dark Séance* (1882) an animated skeleton with rattling jaws lost its head, which floated over the audience. The skeleton was made of papier-mâché, and jointed so that head and limbs could be readily removed and replaced. For this illusion, a costly one to mount, the stage had to be completely hung with black velvet and felt, and the house lights turned low. The conjuror and his props were dressed conspicuously in white, and whatever transformations took place were achieved by an assistant, invisible because he was covered from head to toe in black.

Developments in the field of still photography gave a further boost to the tradition. In-camera tricks meant that ghosts, headless men and doppelgängers could fraternise with the living.

It is obviously technical innovation which gives vitality to the phantasmagoric. The tradition surfaces with new techniques: the development of special effects (optical printing, back projection, glass shots) in the early sound era coincided with films like *White Zombie* (Victor Halperin, 1932) and a host of other phantasmagoric films from the studios of MGM and Universal between 1930 and 1936. Some of John P. Fulton's special effects in *The Invisible Man* (James Whale, 1933) bear a striking resemblance to a method used by Maskelyne: to show the Invisible Man smoking a cigarette, an actor, dressed from head to toe in black, was filmed performing before a black background, then the sequence was optically printed on to footage of the décor, the cigarette appearing to float on air. The animated film, because individual frames are hand-drawn and photographed under the most controlled technical conditions, has been the focus of the phantasmagoric tradition since the metamorphic films of Émile Cohl, "this Méliès of the cartoon".[22] With the coming of sound, Disney and Fleischer were to produce films central to the genre: *The Skeleton Dance* (1930) and *Minnie the Moocher* (1932) respectively.

By 1899, the breadth of Méliès' cinema was beginning to widen. *The Bridegroom's Dilemma* was a stag film; *Murder Will Out* owed something to E. A. Poe; both *Neptune and Amphitrite* and *Christ Walking on the Water* superimposed

Gloria Stuart in a publicity still for *The Invisible Man*.

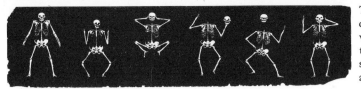

Technical innovation: the choreutoscope. The images were drawn through the lantern in such rapid succession that they appeared to move.

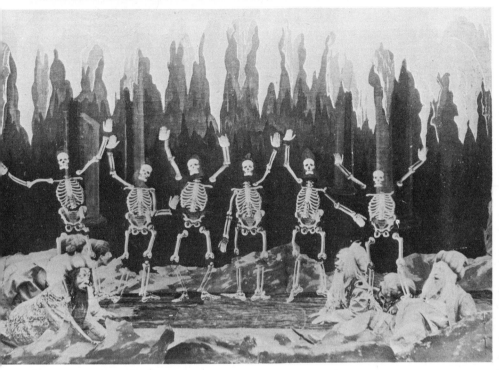

'The Phantoms—A Spectre Combat', scene 18 from Méliès' *The Palace of the Arabian Nights* (1905). The black suits filling out the skeletons' bare bones are just discernible.

Walt Disney, *The Skeleton Dance* (1930).

figures on to images of the sea; *The Mysterious Knight* contained a number of dissolves and *The Lightning Change Artist* presented Frégoli* making twenty character changes in two minutes of film.

A reconstructed newsreel of *The Dreyfus Affair* was Méliès' longest film to date. It was 780 feet and 13 minutes long. The wrongful conviction for high treason of Alfred Dreyfus, a Jewish army officer, and the ensuing agitation for his retrial split French public opinion down the middle. Méliès, who was pro-Dreyfus, based at least some of the eleven sets of his strangely moving film on illustrations in the weekly papers. Dreyfus was played by an ironmonger who bore a strong resemblance to the real man. Other French producers made films of the Dreyfus Affair, Lumière in 1897 and Pathé in 1899.

Méliès' second big production of 1899 was a seven-minute version of *Cinderella* in which "over thirty-five people" (35½?) took part, as the Star Film Catalogue proudly testified. During the year, bi-lingual titles and inscriptions (French/English and later German) became a feature of Star Films. Back in the magic theatre, a revue called *Passez Muscade* (*Hey Presto!*) opened at the Robert-Houdin on April 16, and featured the illusionist Carmelli.

In 1900 Méliès became the president of the Chambre Syndicale des Éditeurs Cinématographiques, an alliance formed at the suggestion of a number of minor French film producers, led by Georges Mendel, to defend their joint interests against the emerging American companies. Méliès was asked to be head of the new group. In assuming such a position, he can have had but a faint intuition of the developments ahead (he was to resign in 1912) and of the economic machinations that were to destroy him.

During 1900 thirty-four Star Films were made. *The Cook's Revenge* was a story of sadism, comedy and vengeance. Méliès himself became every one of the seven musicians in *The One-Man Band*, an idea taken up by Buster Keaton in *The Playhouse* (1921). For the 1900 Exposition Universelle (World's Fair) Méliès made a series of panoramic views of

* Leopoldo Frégoli, an Italian illusionist and quick-change artiste admired by the futurist Marinetti, had been inspired by the Lumières' invention to construct the *Frégoligraphe*, with which he made twenty-six short films whose titles first appear in R. W. Paul's 1897 catalogue. In *Frégoli illusioniste* he made himself disappear and reappear by cutting the film rather than stopping and starting the camera. During *Les Sérénades de Frégoli* he stood behind the screen and recited, in synchronisation, the dialogue of the players.

Cinderella (1899).

The Seven Capital Sins
(1900): 'The Castle of
Pride'.

Paris, and also advertised the activities of the Robert-Houdin
in the official guide. *The Seven Capital Sins* were represented,
of course, by lovely women. *Thanking the Audience* was a
"Special Film for Finishing an Exhibition of Animated
Photography" showing "a clown transforming himself suc-

cessively into a Frenchman, English soldier, German, Spaniard, Italian lady, Russian, and Turkish lady, and thanking the audience by displaying these words: 'Thanks, hope to see you again,' translated into seven different languages."[23] *The Christmas Dream* had dissolving effects, tricks, snow scenes, night scenes, ballets and marches. 'Santa Claus in His Glory' was its apotheosis.

When it came to managing his players, Méliès was a martinet. Astaix, hired to work in the Passage de l'Opéra laboratories, recalled that Méliès always kept his plans to himself, told his workers nothing and was very hard to follow. He appeared to them as an autocrat, as the patron, a strict and fickle father-figure. It seemed that he expected them to understand immediately all the things they had to do and when an actor was not so quick to catch on Méliès would dismiss him, which could lead to ill-feeling. Speed and exactitude were essential, however, for the hours of favourable daylight were few. Tableaux were generally performed at the rate of one or two a week, depending on how complicated and long each was. A big production often demanded two or three months preparation. From the outset Méliès had found it difficult to find players. Rôles in the first films had been taken by family, friends and employees: Méliès' gardener, Louvel, found himself lead player in many of the early films. Eventually, however, he managed to attract dancers from the Châtelet and Opéra to his Montreuil studio. Singers from the café-concert and actors from the Comédie Française soon followed. He gave these artistes one gold louis a day (about 85p) and their dinner. In many of his

Georges Méliès, at right, directing scene 3 of *The Tower of London* (1905), 'The Condemnation'.

films he took the leading rôle himself.

On January 15 1901, Méliès' son, André, was born. A fortnight later the theatre was partially destroyed by a fire which began in a studio above, rented by a photographer named Tourtin. It was redecorated after designs by Méliès: wall paintings of a wizard, an eighteenth-century illusionist and mountebank; pictures on the ceiling of Robert-Houdin's automata; around the cornice were the names of the numerous artistes who had appeared on stage. The cost of rebuilding, which took nine months, was 70.000F, only 24.000F of which was met by insurance. Meanwhile, shows were given at the Salle des Capucines. On September 22 the theatre reopened. Leclerc, cameraman, pianist and inventor, arrested for selling obscene photographs, was replaced by Michaut.

The year's grandest productions were two fairy stories, *Blue Beard* (11 minutes) and *Red Riding Hood* (9 minutes), which featured a young Rachel Gillet and found audiences as far away as Buenos Aires. In *Off to Bloomingdale Asylum*, or *Off to Bedlam* as it was called in the u.k.,

an omnibus arrives drawn by an extraordinary mechanical horse. On the top are four negroes. The horse kicks and upsets the negroes, who are changed into white clowns. They slap each other's faces and by the blows become black again. They kick each other and become white once more. Finally, they are all merged into one large negro, and when he refuses to pay his carfare, the conductor sets fire to the omnibus and the negro bursts into a thousand pieces.[24]

Blue Beard (1901). Scene 5, 'The Forbidden Chamber'. Bluette Bernon has the key and Jehanne d'Alcy (the second Mme Méliès) is the corpse on the right. There is a pool of 'blood' on the stage.

Red Riding Hood (1901).
Scene 10, 'The Steep
Rocks and Waterfall'
with Méliès at right.

Off to Bloomingdale Asylum
(1901). Scatological
drawing by Méliès.

The mêlée between black and white recalls the tussle between the miller with a sack of flour and the chimney-sweep
with a bag of soot which was a favourite music-hall turn of
the day. The English director George A. Smith made a film
version of such a confrontation, *The Miller and the Sweep*
(1898). The joke was still worth a laugh in 1933 when James
Whale used it in *The Invisible Man*, in which a white cat is

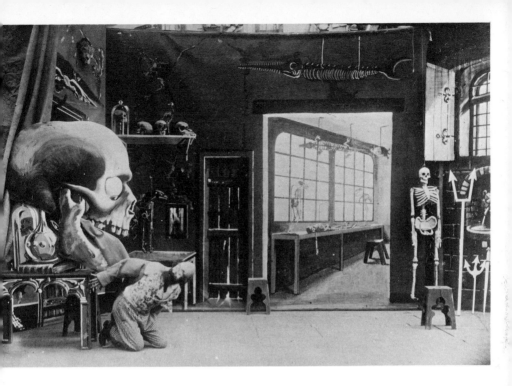

turned into a black cat by a policeman with a paint-spray who takes it for the invisible Claude Rains. Whale's film has an air of buffoonery and vaudeville, which must have come from his early career in the provincial English theatre. That theatre was, presumably, not unknown to Méliès.

Because in 1901 orthochromatic film emulsions created false photographic values—blue becomes white, red and yellow becomes black—décors, costumes and make-up were composed of tones of grey (grisaille). Sets were based on sketches and maquettes made by Méliès, constructed of wood and canvas, sized, and decorated by artists like Claudel, Parvillier and Lecuit-Monroy according to the aesthetic of scenery painting, with its emphasis on perspective and *trompe-l'œil*. Accessories were constructed of wood, canvas, cardboard, clay and plaster. Chairs, tables, carpets, candelabra, clocks, fireplaces and all kinds of furniture were specially made and painted in grisaille.

Some of Méliès' more spectacular black-and-white subjects were transformed into colour films at the studio of Mme Thuillier, where a team of women, each assigned a colour, hand-tinted them frame by frame. The transparent aniline colours were diluted in water and alcohol. With

The set of *The Phrenologist and the Lively Skull* (1901). The power of this image resides in the dialogue between the real and illusory perspective of the three-dimensional props, the two-dimensional cut-outs and the painted back-cloth, grisaille being the common denominator.

Mlle Rouillon, Mme Vallouy and M. Fornelio, Mme Thuillier was responsible for the whole French industry, although some fairground showmen coloured their copies themselves to save money. The cost of tinting approximately doubled the price of a film. To buy *Joan of Arc* (813 feet) plain cost £45, but £80 coloured; a plain *Gulliver's Travels* (280 feet) came to £7.50, a coloured one £15. Over the years the margin grew wider as the cost of colouring increased. By 1907 colouring had almost trebled the price of a film like *Tunnelling the English Channel*: a black-and-white print cost $120, a coloured print $320. Pathé eventually developed a cheaper, mechanical method of colouring using stencils in about 1905. Colour had its decorative qualities but Méliès used it for trick value too. To show a conjuror effortlessly changing clothes he instructed Mme Thuillier to vary their colours: a red jacket became a yellow, then a green, then a violet one.

Gaston Méliès in Algeria a year before his death in 1915.

Due to the wholesale counterfeiting of his films in the U.S.A. where, distributed till February 1904 by the American Mutoscope and Biograph Company, they had found great

popularity, Méliès decided to open his own office in New
York to protect his interests. Putting the Star Film trademark on every frame had proved useless: would-be pirates
like Siegmund Lubin simply erased it from their duped
prints. In November 1902 Georges' fifty-year-old brother,
Gaston, set sail for New York, where he opened the Star
Film Agency at 204 E 38 Street: "In opening a factory and
office in New York we are prepared and determined ener-
getically to pursue all counterfeiters and pirates. We will not
speak twice, we will act!"[25]

Gaston Méliès, the author of those lines, had fallen on
hard times. Between October 1890 and spring 1894 he and
his brother Henri had rented an office in London, at Imperial
Mansions, 178 Charing Cross Road (where the notorious
Centre Point skyscraper now stands), from where they sold
footware. In 1893 Gaston secured a six-and-a-half-year contract to supply boots to the military in the 2nd and 3rd
arrondissements of Paris. In January 1895 a sharp increase
in the price of leather ruined him; on August 12 1895, the
contract was cancelled by the Ministry of War.

As the import of positive film was heavily taxed in the
U.S.A. Méliès began in 1902 to make two negatives of every
film, using a second camera, one negative being shipped to
New York. In *The Man With the Rubber Head* a chemist in his
laboratory blows up a head exactly like his own with a pair
of bellows until it is as big as he is. Eventually the head
explodes in a great puff of smoke. It was Méliès' own head
and to make it grow he sat on a movable dolly that was
drawn towards the camera, a screen hiding his body and the
machinery. Expansion and diminution were motifs in *The
Devil and the Statue, The Dwarf and the Giant, The Dancing*

The Devil and the Statue
(1902). Méliès as Satan.

The Man With the Rubber Head (1902). A drawing by Méliès of his head exploding.

The Eruption of Mount Pelee (1902). Pyrotechnic effects and model-making in a reconstructed newsreel.

Midget and *The Elastic Battalion*, although for these films Méliès moved the camera, not the subject, photographing figures on a black background using a forward or reverse tracking shot. In *The Prolific Magical Egg* he used a fade to

change himself from a magician into a skeleton. *Up-to-Date Surgery* contains a mad doctor who, diagnosing acute indigestion, chops his patient up into little pieces and then reassembles the bits in the wrong order. After the necessary adjustments are made the patient, entirely cured, departs from the surgery in high spirits.

A Trip to the Moon (1902). Scene 4, 'The Foundries. The Chimney-stacks. The Casting of the Monster Gun'.

In May Méliès made two reconstructed newsreels using models: *The Eruption of Mount Pelee* (Martinique) in which flour erupts from a plaster volcano, and *The Catastrophe of the Balloon 'Pax'*. In *The Human Fly* a man walked on a floor made to look like a ceiling while the film was shot upside-down, an idea used by R. W. Paul in *Upside Down*, which was directed by Walter R. Booth in 1898. During the same month of May, Méliès made *A Trip to the Moon*. This space-opera, lasting 14 minutes with 30 scenes, is a parody of Verne's and Wells' lunar novels, and a far cry from the reserve and didacticism of *From the Earth to the Moon* (1865) and *The First Men in the Moon* (1901). Méliès was producer, director, scriptwriter, set designer, costumier and lead actor. Other roles were taken by Victor André, Henri Delannoy,

A Trip to the Moon (1902). Right: Drawing by Méliès of scene 6 (not scene 5 as he has written): 'Loading the Gun'.

A Trip to the Moon (1902).
Scene 21, 'The Departure
From the Moon'.
A Selenite hangs on.
Below right: Scene 9,
'Landed Right in the
Eye!!!'

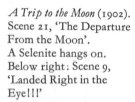

Red Grooms' expression-
istic Man in the Moon,
from Rudy Burckhardt's
homage to Méliès, *Shoot
the Moon* (1962). Méliès
and the underground
film-maker of today
share an artisanal status.

Robinson Crusoe (1902).
Scene 3, 'His Progress Up
the River'. Méliès/Crusoe
transports a Star Film
copyright notice along
with the bare essentials of
life.

Farjaux, Kelm and Brunnet (the astronauts); Bluette Bernon sat on the crescent moon; the stars and gunners were dancers from the Châtelet; and the Selenites were played by acrobats from the Folies-Bergère. *A Trip to the Moon* was to achieve world-wide success and is today perhaps the most famous of his films. Méliès did not think it one of his best.

The year's longest film, *Robinson Crusoe* (15 minutes), based on a pantomime presented at the Châtelet during the winter of 1899, had a spectacular thunderstorm in it, electric lights providing the lightning. During the film's apotheosis a dissolve takes the audience back through time and space, from Robinson Crusoe's parlour, where he has been reunited with his family, to Crusoe and Man Friday's defence of their hut against marauding cannibals.

The Coronation of Edward VII, a newsreel reconstructed *before* the event, was commissioned by Charles Urban, the director of the Warwick Trading Company and, since 1900, Star Film's British agent. Urban, an American entrepreneur who dominated the pre-war British film industry, had come to London in 1896 as the manager of Maguire and Baucus, a company marketing Edison films. In April 1897 the company was renamed the Warwick Trading Company and, until the American broke away in 1903 to form the Charles Urban Trading Company (taking the Star Film account with him), it showed substantial yearly profits. Urban and Méliès worked hand in glove: each was the other's agent in their respective countries. Even though Urban made a number of 'donations' to an official at H.M. Office of Works he was unable to secure permission to film inside Westminster Abbey. Urban was undaunted. He commissioned his French colleague to reconstruct the coronation and duly sent Méliès pictures of the Abbey, and the costumes and accessories that were to be used in the ceremony. Subsequently he travelled to Montreuil to vet Méliès' project. The existence in Urban's own scrapbook of an undated brochure pertaining to an enormous oil painting of the coronation by Edwin Austin Abbey R.A. suggests that this picture could have served as a model for Méliès' own designs. Alas, the painting was not begun until shortly after the ceremony, and was not completed until 1904: it has no bearing on the Méliès/Urban collaboration. The Star Film King Edward was played by a communal wash-house attendant, his queen by a singer from the Châtelet. Due to Edward's ill-health the actual coronation was postponed from June to August 9. The lengthy ceremony was reduced to a six-minute film, which

Charles Urban.

Urban's Phonograph and Kinetoscope Parlor in Detroit, 1895.

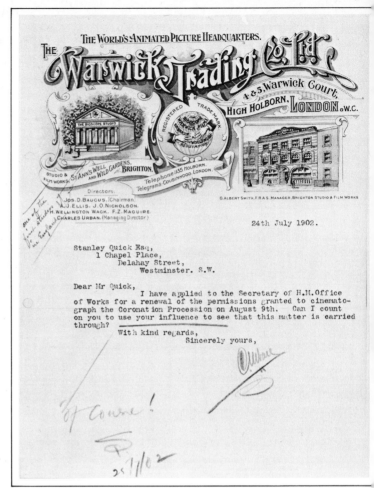

Because of the postponement of the coronation Urban had to reapply for permission to film the procession.

was inserted between footage, shot by Urban, of the royal coach arriving and departing from Westminster. It was shown on the evening of Coronation Day at the Alhambra music-hall in Leicester Square, where Urban films formed a regular part of the programme.

By 1903 Star Film had agents in Berlin, Barcelona, London, and in New York, where Gaston Méliès was joined by his son, Paul. To copyright them, paper prints of Méliès' films were deposited in the Library of Congress, Washington, beginning in June. This practice ceased in May 1904 after thirty-three prints had been deposited. Méliès did, however, continue registering films with the Copyright Office until late 1909. On August 22 1903, Gaston Méliès made his first film, a newsreel called *The Yacht Race* (*Reliance–Shamrock*

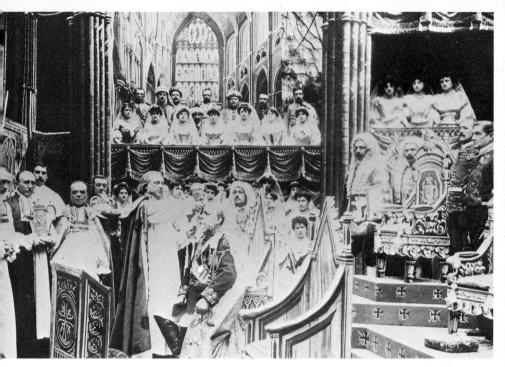

III). Meanwhile, in Paris, three of Méliès' employees, Michaut, Astaix and Lallement, left to form a distribution agency, American Kinema.

Georges' shortest film in 1903 was *The Enchanted Basket*, one and-a-half minutes long, about a man battling with a demon, and the longest was *Fairyland, or the Kingdom of the Fairies*, 18 minutes long and a tale of abduction and rescue, with a witch who disappears in a pillar of fire, a princess who sleeps in a shell-shaped bed, submarine grottoes, and a prince who rides a sturgeon. Real water, agitated mechanically (in the manner of *Divers at Work on the Wreck of the 'Maine'* of 1898) or sprinkled as rain, was used in several scenes. Water from *The Enchanted Well* became fire. In *The Melomaniac*,

In this publicity shot from *The Coronation of Edward VII* the painted flat representing the nave has not been put back into its normal position, and a wall with creepers on it can be glimpsed in the gap. The presence of the wall suggests that the film was shot out of doors.

a singing teacher, followed by his pupils, runs across some telegraph wires strung on poles. These five wires, the professor thinks, would form a very effective musical 'staff'. He carries an enormous 'key of G', which he throws upon the wires to give the proper 'pitch' to his pupils. He forms a 'measure' by fixing his stick in a perpendicular position among the wires. In order to have notes, he tears off his own head, and fixes it among the wires. Thus he obtains the first note of his air. Then he

The Melomaniac (1903).
Méliès as music teacher
and his head as crotchets.

fixes upon this 'staff' several heads corresponding in position to the first part of the tune 'God Save the King'. On
the beating of drums the heads rearrange themselves, and
one sees the second line of the air. Another beating of
drums, and the heads shift about until they form the third
line of music. Satisfied, the professor departs followed by
his pupils. The heads, abandoned among the wires, cast
a look at the crowd as it disappears. Immediately the heads
are transformed to birds and fly away.[26]

It is interesting to note that the illustrator and caricaturist
J. J. Grandville, whose metamorphic drawings were, so to
speak, 'animated' by Méliès and Émile Cohl, published a
series of humorous scores in which musical notes form the
heads of Turkish warriors, dancers and penitents, in the
popular journal *Le Magasin pittoresque*, in about 1840.

In *Jack Jaggs and Dum Dum* a magician treats a man as if he
were a nail, using a hammer on the man's head to drive him
into the stage. Dissolves upon a white rather than black
ground were the innovation of *A Spiritualistic Photographer*
and *The Magic Lantern*, made shortly afterwards. To achieve
this effect Méliès must have opened, rather than closed, the
diaphragm of the camera-lens. A new trick was introduced
with *The Apparition, or Mr. Jones' Comical Experience With
a Ghost*. A traveller, suffering from hallucinations, sees a
phantom grow indistinct then clear (focus), become transparent then opaque (exposure), and "enter into the most
marvellous vibrations, horizontal and vertical".[27] *Jupiter's
Thunderbolts* was a mythological burlesque. Mlle Zizi Papillon

performed an "eccentric" dance in *The Ballet-Master's Dream.*
The Condemnation of Faust, 8 minutes long and in sixteen
scenes "with diabolical trimmings", was inspired by Berlioz.
It took the audience on a journey through the mineral world,
via rock, water, ice, crystal and fire.

For Méliès the scenario had little importance. He preferred
to invent details first of all, out of which a final narrative
developed. He liked to include a few tricks—"one trick leads
to another", he once said—then one principal grandiose effect
and a final apotheosis. "You could say that the scenario is in
this case simply a thread intended to link the 'effects', in
themselves without much relation to each other. I mean to
say that the scenario has no more than a secondary importance in this genre of composition . . . I was appealing to
the spectator's eyes alone, trying to charm and intrigue him,
hence the scenario was of no importance."[28] One is reminded
of Nevil Maskelyne's words on magical items: "beads held
together and supported by the thread of dramatic interest".
These 'effects', or 'beads'—tricks, sets, costumes and props—
were hastily scribbled down on any available bit of paper.
Méliès, painter manqué and political caricaturist, always
sketched in the same way, beginning in a corner of the
paper, exactly like Henri Rousseau, with whom he has much
in common.

The matte processes used rendering it 'objective', Méliès'
camera seemed to remain as still and sedate as a spectator
seated in an auditorium. His films are essentially photographed pantomimes. This is no pejorative observation: for
Méliès the movie camera was a mechanism that permitted his
tricks and tableaux to be seen in numerous theatres at once.
The cinema had "exhibition value".[29] It was a form of
printing. Of course, he did not think it was that alone—
indeed, he pioneered a number of purely cinematic tricks
within the theatrical context he'd chosen to work in. Méliès
used the medium of film in a practical way, to enable himself
to become a better conjuror:

In conjuring you work under the attentive gaze of the
public, who never fail to spot a suspicious movement. You
are alone, their eyes never leave you. Failure would not be
tolerated . . . While in the cinema . . . you can do your
confecting quietly, far from those profane gazes, and you
can do things thirty-six times if necessary until they are
right. This allows you to travel further in the domain of
the marvellous."[30]

Minutes of the Chambre
Syndicale de la Presti-
digitation (1904–55), in
two volumes.

The Barber of Sevilla (1904).

On May 24 1904, Méliès was elected president of the Chambre Syndicale de la Prestidigitation. (He was already president of the Chambre Syndicale des Éditeurs Cinématographiques.) This new union, which imitated the operative masonic orders of the day, had grown out of the Académie de Prestidigitation, founded by Méliès in 1891 to fight for a better reception for itinerant illusionists from the municipalities in which they desired to work. The Isola brothers, wealthy theatre-owners, were honorary presidents of the union, and Raynaly, an illusionist who appeared regularly at the Robert-Houdin, was vice-president. The Chambre Syndicale met regularly, usually on every fourth Thursday, until 1934 (and briefly in 1951 and 1955), except for a period between May 1914 and April 1920. Freemasonry and conjuring share a common renaissance in the eighteenth century and a number of other characteristics: a feeling for ritual, a fixed symbolism and the need for secrecy.

The year 1904 produced three major films. *Faust and Marguerite* was intended to be projected in synchronisation with the principal airs of Gounod's opera, and could be shown in conjunction with *The Damnation of Faust* (1903). Méliès had been selling specially composed sheet music with his films since 1900. *The Barber of Sevilla* [*sic*], 22 minutes in length, but also available in a shortened version (as were a number of Méliès' longer films), was based on the play by Beaumarchais. Led by the engineer Crazyloff, a team of savants, including Professor Polehunter, Secretary Rattlebrains, and Officers Easy-fooled, Daredevil and Schemer, made *An Impossible Voyage* of 24 minutes through earth, air, fire and water, from the rooms of the Institute of Incoherent Geography (an antecedent of the College of 'Pataphysics) to the surface of the sun then back to the bottom of the ocean. Méliès suggested the illusion of both aerial and terrestrial speed by filming the painted side of a rotating drum and then superimposing Crazyloff's aircraft on to it, a device known as the 'follow shot'. A supplementary section of three scenes, each a minute long, was available, in which Crazyloff uses an enormous electro-magnet to recover a car lost in Switzerland, a train lost in the sun and a submarine lost in the sea. In *Every Man His Own Cigar Lighter*, an English tourist unable to obtain a match to light his cigar creates a double to do it for him. A chef literally stews in his own juice in *The Cook In Trouble*. Only his tattered garments are recovered from the pot into which he fell.

1905 was a year of expansion: thousands of costumes were

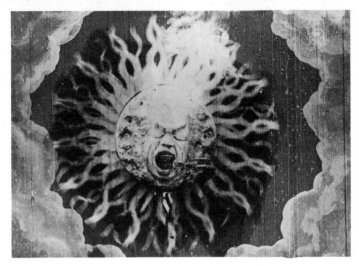

An Impossible Voyage (1904). Scene 21, 'A Nauseous Pill'. The sun is about to swallow a flying train.

bought when the Maison Lepère went into liquidation; Méliès installed electric lighting in his studio to augment the peevish sunlight he used for filming; a second studio was built at Montreuil, on the Rue Galliéni, and put in the charge of the actor Manuel. And yet 1905* is the year that marks the beginning of Méliès' decline. It may even be that the year's 'investments' speeded it up.

On December 6 the centenary of J. E. Robert-Houdin's birth was celebrated at the theatre, when conjurors Legris, Folletto, Caroly, Raynaly, Talazac and Michaëlla, De Cago (otherwise known as 'The Marquis of O') and Zirka performed.

The Christmas Angel, "a grand picture of Pathos and Humour with a Moral", was a rare excursion into film melodrama. Méliès tended to avoid the moralising and chauvinistic subjects preferred by many of his contemporaries. Scene 3, 'The Midnight Mass', gives a good idea of this production, a work of social criticism that takes on overtones of Buñuel:

> The steps of the Church are covered with professional beggars who wait for the devout worshippers to come out,

---

* "The tremendous vogue for the marvellous seems to be over by 1905, and it is not by chance that one sees the director of an important establishment like Kétorza trying to sell second-hand, at a low price, 'three fairy films by the Maison Méliès, in a new condition, *Cinderella, Blue Beard, Robinson Crusoe*, at one franc a metre, 10% discount on the three.' Four months later the films were still for sale . . ." (Jacques Deslandes and Jacques Richard, *Histoire comparée du cinéma*, Tome II, p. 221).

The Christmas Angel
(1905). Rachel Gillet and
Georges Méliès.

since they are almost always generous on this day. Little
Marie comes and takes her place among them, but the
others drive her away, threatening her with their sticks
and crutches. The poor child, overcome with fatigue, goes
and sits down at the foot of the lamp post. Soon out come
the worshippers who give their alms to the professional
beggars; footmen and grooms carry the umbrellas and
cloaks for the ladies. Poor little Marie holds out her hand
timidly but is refused by all, their patience having been
worn out by the solicitations of the other beggars. One
gentleman whom she follows in despair bullies her and
strikes her violently. She falls on her knees bleeding.[31]

'The Snow Drops', dancers from the London Alhambra,
performed in *A Mesmerian Experiment*. *A Crazy Composer* has
Mr Bang-the-Box, in despair at not being able to write any
decent music, commit suicide by shoving his head into his
piano, which explodes. *An Adventurous Automobile Trip* had
been made in 1904 to figure in a revue at the Folies-Bergère,
written by Victor de Cottens. When the revue ended after
three hundred performances Méliès put his film up for sale.
De Cottens made a guest appearance in it. Doctor Death-
cheater lived up to his name in *Life-Saving Up-to-Date*. The

story of Ulysses, Calypso and Polyphemus was recounted in *Life and Work*
The Mysterious Island. [61]

Late in 1905 Gaston Méliès in New York had announced
that the retail price of Star Film would be reduced, as of
February 1 1906, from 15 cents to 12 cents per foot. This
measure had positive results: in November 1906 profits in
the U.S.A. amounted to $964; by January 1907 to $2,444;
and in March 1907 they were at $1,921.

The Chimney Sweep, made in March 1906, "an extravagant
'cock and bull' story in 25 scenes",[32] was about the world of
reality assuming, through good fortune, the idealised splen-
dour of a dreamed world. Two duellists managed to wound
or kill six onlookers without suffering a scratch themselves

A Desperate Crime (1906).
Scene 8, 'The House on
Fire'. Shot out of doors.

A Desperate Crime (1906).
Scene 26, 'Last Resist-
ance'.

in *Who Looks, Pays*. In *A Desperate Crime*, a murderer is caught, tried and guillotined for the brutal slaying of a farmer and his family. Some scenes were shot out-of-doors in the grounds of Méliès' villa. The Star Film Catalogue announced that three lithographs depicting the drama had been made by the Donaldson Lithographing Company* of Newport, Kentucky, as well as "an excellent half-sheet" made by Hennegan & Co. of Cincinnati, Ohio.

In *Soap Bubbles* Méliès the conjuror blew bubbles with girls' faces in them that developed into butterfly-women. As a finale he turned himself into a soap bubble and floated away. *The Merry Frolics of Satan* was built around a number of tableaux that Méliès had filmed to link scenes of a pantomime by Victor Darlay and Victor de Cottens, *The Merry Deeds of Satan*, which opened at the Châtelet on December 23 1905: "O enchantment of memories!" wrote de Cottens. "Marvels: like at the Châtelet of old, where I used to wave the magic wand that could change shepherdesses into princesses and a thatched cottage into a castle."[33] To the seven tableaux of a fantastic aerial trip and a cyclone Méliès added twenty-three other scenes, completely different from the Châtelet production. An English engineer, William Crackford, visits Satan's laboratory where he signs a pact with the Devil who, in return for his soul, supplies him with some enchanted pills that can make whatever the engineer desires appear. Crackford ends up on Satan's turnspit. The Devil's lab looks like the inside of a skull with the cupola forming a cranium, a corkscrew chimney the ear's cochlea, and a huge telescope the eye. The 'horse' in Max Ernst's frottage *The Beautiful Season* (1925) looks very much like 'The Skidoo Horse' (scene 19): similar artists with similar visions. In November Méliès made *The Witch*, based on a Breton folk-tale, and featuring talismans, magic potions, monsters, and "a nuptial kiss".

Méliès had created no new theatrical tricks between 1897 and 1905, but by 1907 illusions on stage were occupying him at the expense of his cinematic activities. One such presentation, *Spirit Phenomena*, was performed in September 1907, and showed a bewildered medium visited by a phantom: "a final spectre materialises on stage. This one has more familiar charms. Seating itself on the knee of the terrified medium it half undresses him . . . but it is punished for its temerity by

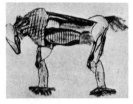

Max Ernst's frottage, *The Beautiful Season* (1925).

Legris struggling against a stage phantom in *Spirit Phenomena* (1907).

* By a curious coincidence (?) the Star Film Trading Company set up in London in 1908 found itself in premises adjacent to the Donaldson Lithographing Company.

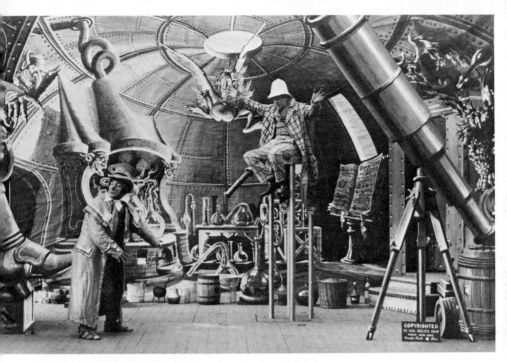

The Merry Frolics of Satan (1906). Scene 3, 'The Laboratory of Satan'.

The Merry Frolics of Satan (1906). 'The Skidoo Horse'. The ropes and machinery for animating this puppet horse and coach can be seen against the black background.

a brisk dematerialisation between the pages of a pretty thick prayer book, from which it cannot re-emerge."[34] On behalf of the conjurors' union its president Georges Méliès sent a reproof to the escapologist Houdini, who had lately been publicly slandering Robert-Houdin, yet whose name he had been happy to 'borrow' and adapt.

Foul-smelling cheeses attack and asphyxiate several policemen and a magistrate in *The Skipping Cheeses*: the cheese-monger, in court because the smell of her wares has offended her fellow-passengers, has absolute power over the recalcitrant savouries, which return to her basket after doing their dirty work. A man is choked to death by the fumes rising from an old pair of shoes in *A New Death Penalty*.

Under the Seas is a lampoon of Jules Verne's *Twenty Thousand Leagues Under the Sea* (1870). Yves the fisherman dreams of a submarine trip to the sea-bed, where he meets marine monsters, the Queen of the Starfish, mermaids, naiads (danced by the *corps de ballet* from the Châtelet, directed by Mme Stichel) and where he is attacked by sea anemones, corals, an octopus and a vicious sponge before he wakes up. The marine creatures in *Under the Seas* are painted cut-outs based directly on a number of illustrations by Alphonse de Neuville in Verne's novel.* The humorous excesses of Méliès contrast strikingly with Verne's sober narrative, and his espousal of technology and imperialism.

A Mischievous Sketch had a logic all of its own:

An easel appears, and soon after a canvas 'walks' up from the floor of its own accord and takes its place on the easel. Now an artist's portfolio is seen; it opens up and different parts of a sketch which are enclosed therein mysteriously fly from it upon the canvas until finally all the parts resemble the image of a man. When completed the picture becomes animated and comes down on to the ground and engages in some merry antics with its own skeleton which shortly after is changed into a lady. After frolicking around for an interval the man is changed to a sketch on the canvas; then it begins to dismember itself, one portion at a time. After all the parts of the sketch are in the portfolio, it folds itself up; then the animated person appears from some mysterious source and carries off the portfolio in which his own image is enclosed.[35]

The Eclipse was full of *double entendre*: "The 'man in the sun' is at one end of the heaven and dainty Diana at the other; they move toward each other until the sun is eclipsed, at which Diana shows her approval by a series of ecstatic facial expressions; then they move on once more."[36] Later in the year Méliès raced through *Hamlet, Prince of Denmark* in nine-and-a-half minutes, and made a film of *Shakespeare*

* Karel Zeman, the Czech animator, used enlargements of the illustrations from Verne's books as settings for *The Wonderful Invention* (1958) and *On The Comet* (1970).

Under the Seas (1907).
Scene 6, 'Military
Honours'.

Under the Seas (1907). Set
for scene 21, 'Crabs and
Monstrous Fish'. (left)
Close examination of
the two illustrations
from Jules Verne's
*Twenty Thousand Leagues
Under the Sea* will reveal
the source of the majority
of Méliès' marine
monsters.

The Eclipse (1907). An
astronomy professor
meets with a fatal
accident.

Writing 'Julius Caesar', a task the playwright apparently performed with some passion.

By 1908 cartels, not castles, were in the air. The industry had developed to a point propitious for amalgamation. A committee set up in Paris in the spring of that year and presided over by Méliès set the date for the founding congress of the newly-formed Association International des Fabricants de Films for November 18. News, presumably of a similar American project, led to the dropping of this course of action. Nevertheless, a preparatory assembly was held in the headquarters of the Éclair Company at which an attempt was made by Gaumont to establish a single tariff for the sale of films, which were sold by the metre at this time. Méliès, who spared no expense on his productions,* and had the most to lose, used his influence to put a stop to the idea. Dramatic commercial developments just around the corner were to render the question completely irrelevant. Yet in August 1908 the short-lived Star Film Trading Company was set up in London at 7 Rupert Court, off Rupert Street, Soho, and put under the management of James M. Dounie,† an indication that Méliès still felt the future held promise.

The period from 1903 to 1908 marks a transition in the cinema from petty commerce to big business, from the artisanal to the capitalist organisation it has largely remained. We have seen that it was Méliès himself who was largely instrumental in setting up the earliest corporation of minor French producers concerned with protecting their interests against emergent American competition. But the Chambre Syndicale des Éditeurs Cinématographiques was essentially a *defensive* unit: the notion of domination of a world market (which was in an embryonic state in 1900 anyway) was far from the mind of the men who set it up. The growth of the industry at this time coincides with an era of imperialist expansion leading to the First World War, with the emergence of giant trusts and combines, and the growing dominance of finance capital, and is exemplified by the appearance, in the U.S.A., of the Motion Picture Patents Company (M.P.P.C.), set up by Edison in January 1908. The

---

* "Don't forget that my films are the most expensive of all, for only well-wrought pictures are made by me, necessitating sound direction, costly décors and costumes, and a lot of hard work to succeed on account of the tricks in them."

(George Méliès, letter of February 6 1906)

† Might James Dounie be the J. Downey who, with F. Downey, exhibited 'Downey's Living Photographs' in the north of England in 1896?

M.P.P.C. wanted to stabilise and control the American market. It had an exclusive contract with Eastman's Kodak Company to supply raw stock. Theatres were to be classified and licensed to show the company's films on the company's patented equipment. Méliès, represented by Gaston, joined up: the only other French producer to register was Pathé. The American companies represented were Edison, Biograph, Vitagraph, Essanay, Selig, Lubin, Kalem, and the distributor, George Kleine. As a result of the company's repressive policies, independents sprang up and defected to the other side of the continent, to Hollywood, to make their films. In 1910 the M.P.P.C. set up a national film exchange, the General Film Company, and bought out all but one firm, William Fox's. Fox, whose position was strengthened by the determination of another independent, Carl Laemmle, eventually sued the company and won. By 1914 the M.P.P.C. was all but defunct.

Méliès undertook to supply the American market with the massive sum of 300 metres (1,000 feet) ·of film per week. Later in 1908, Gaston Méliès formed a production company in Chicago, the Méliès Manufacturing Company, to aid in supplying this quota. Set up in September 1908 with assets of $75,000, the company's headquarters were at the Criterion Theatre.

Towards the end of 1907 Méliès had made a picture called *Delirium In a Studio*: it is a title that aptly describes the absolute frenzy in which he must have produced 1908's colossal output, which amounted to sixty-eight films lasting roughly ten hours, a sum equal to the aggregate of work produced between 1896 and 1903. He was under extreme and often desperate pressure, as some of this year's sardonic pictures show. *Humanity Through The Ages*, for example, is an ironical anthology of crime and brutality. The penultimate scene shows the delegates of the 1907 Hague Conference, convened to limit arms and armies, coming to blows. The last scene, mordantly titled 'Triumph', shows us the results of the peace conference: a battlefield strewn with dead and wounded soldiers over which looms the Angel of Destruction. *A Fake-Diamond Swindler* was a satirical reconstructed newsreel about a hoaxer called Lemoine who had claimed he could manufacture gems. The film's French title punned on the hoaxer's name, *L'Habit ne fait pas le moine* ('the habit doesn't make the monk', or 'clothes (do not) make the man'). *Mishaps of the N.Y.–Paris Race* was a sarcastic travelogue, a spiritual companion of Alfred Jarry's story *The Supermale*

Humanity Through the Ages (1908). Scene 11, 'The Triumph of the Peace Congress'.

(1902), its target being an actual race organised by an American magazine. *In the Bogie Man's Cave*, an oedipal fantasy about oral aggression, shows an ogre chopping up a little boy and eating him.

Fairy stories and comedies full of pranks and practical jokes accounted for much of the year's output. *Grandmother's Story* and *La Fée libellule* were fairy tales; *Curiosity Punished* and *A Night With Masqueraders In Paris* were comedies. In *Fun With the Bridal Party* chairs move because they are controlled by strings pulled by two pranksters who become 'ghosts' when they cover themselves with white sheets. In *Incident From Don Quixote* the dreamy hero

is found fighting reptiles of his imagination. When he has disposed of them, his armour, which he has laid aside, seems to have become inhabited by a peculiar being with limbs that stretch yards in length. The armour then falls to the ground and a beautiful maiden is disclosed. She suddenly becomes a butterfly, and as the knight approaches her the wings of the butterfly give way to the huge tentacles of a giant spider or octopus, which reach out for

Grandmother's Story (1908). Shot on a lawn.

Don Quixote and try to grasp him. He reaches for his spear, but it fades from view, and he awakens only to find himself savagely attacking Sancho Panza, his faithful but luckless man servant.[37]

The year 1909 marks the final turning-point in the career of Georges Méliès. From 2–4 February he presided at the International Convention of Cinematograph Editors, held at the offices of the Société Française de Photographie et de Cinématographie, 51 Rue de Clichy, at which fifty delegates, representing the seven nations then producing films, were present. Two of the most powerful men in the cinema world dominated the congress: George Eastman and Charles Pathé. Méliès proposed that the perforation of films be internationally unified,* but the major decision taken, mooted by Pathé, was that the practice of selling films be replaced by hiring them out for periods of four months, at the fixed tariff of 1,25F per metre.

Pathé's plan was to stabilise and control the French and

* "I love the idea of a man impassioned as much about the problem of perforation as about a trip to the moon." (Norman McLaren, 1954).

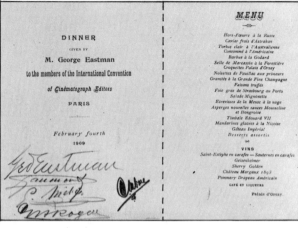

Cover of the menu of a dinner given by George Eastman on the final day of the International Congress of Cinematograph Editors. Pathé's familiar trademark, the cock, figures strongly in the drawing, just as he did at the congress. The menu has been autographed by Eastman, Gaumont, Méliès, Rogers and Urban.

European markets. This commercial adjustment would lead to standardisation and would encourage the mass-production and uniformity of films, and their more rapid turnover. The inevitable intercession of the film exchange would abet the bureaucratisation of the industry. These were innovations that spelled trouble for Méliès, who had financed and made films independent of such restrictions. He had, in the past, been approached by Claude Grivolas, an industrialist with a large interest in the Pathé Company and a member of the Chambre Syndicale de la Prestidigitation, and by Clément-Maurice, on behalf of the Éclair Company. Both organisations had sought an alliance with Star Film. On each occasion Méliès, who was then a much bigger fish, had declined, preferring to remain independent and finance films with his own (diminishing) funds. He was simply unaware—or too proud to admit—that his artisanal status would lead to his demise unless he gave it up to join one of the developing capitalistic enterprises.

The fairground showmen, Méliès' principal clients, were badly shaken by the news. Since 1905, competition from permanent urban cinemas, rising transport costs, arbitrary taxation and dishonest dealings had brought about a decline in this sector of the entertainment industry. It was in a condition too fragile to withstand another blow: this radical change was the last straw. The fairground artisans saw themselves being pushed out of the market by a gang of big business-men. Méliès, placed in a difficult position, tried to explain:

> The new ruling has the sole purpose of preventing a depreciation in prices to a level where neither producers nor exhibitors could make a living. I am one of the oldest

established producers . . . For more than twelve years now
I have produced a considerable body of work and I am
sure that nobody would take me for an *exploiter* living the
easy life with his hands in his pockets all day. I am not in
partnership. I am an independent producer. We estimate
that a year will be necessary to clear stocks, interest and
past errors, to deliver the market from scratched and
shoddy films, to encourage the lowering of entry prices, so
that the exhibitions that result will cause our profession
to become again what it used to be: an artistic one, that
can subsist and do well.[38]

Historically speaking, Méliès' days were as numbered as the
fairground showmen's were.

A fairground cinema.

As the fortune of Pathé grew the fortunes of Méliès declined. Pathé had made his money by assiduously exploiting
Edison's phonograph and *Kinetoscope* in the fairgrounds near
Paris. In 1896 he went into films, bringing little originality
to the new medium: his 1899 catalogue looks like the 1896
one of Lumière and Méliès. In 1900 he put Ferdinand Zecca,
who was to specialise in melodramas, in charge of production. To direct trick films and fairy stories Pathé hired
Gaston Velle, the son of a conjuror who had in his time
appeared at the Théâtre Robert-Houdin. Lucien Nonguet,
noted as a director of crowd scenes, made a contribution
also. Méliès must have noted with consternation the building
of a Pathé studio near his own in Montreuil in 1903. Five
years later the Société Pathé, heavily backed by French
finance capital, was expanding rapidly. Indeed, by 1908
Pathé was the world's largest producer of films, turning out
four times as much as his nearest French rival, Gaumont.
Méliès was nowhere in sight.

The commercial crisis precipitated by the decision to rent film rather than sell it so affected Méliès that he was unable to make a picture until the autumn of 1909. His films were not doing so well in the U.S.A.* By the time winter came round Méliès had turned his attention to the theatre, for he had been commissioned to mount an adaptation of one of his theatrical productions, *Spirit Phenomena*, at the Folies-Bergère. Lack of information makes the job of dating films during 1909 and 1910 a difficult one. *Cinderella Up-to-Date*, released in October 1909, is a comedy in which a lot of old maids try to emulate a Cinderella who, they have read in the newspapers, fell for the man who found her lost shoe. A suffragette is satirised in *Mrs and Mr Duff*. With the Salvation Army girl she proved to be a favourite butt for Méliès' humour.

The French market must have stabilised somewhat by 1910, for Méliès produced fifteen films that year. Recently discovered letters from P. Tainguy, Méliès' business manager, to Léon Gaumont tell us that Star Films were then distributed through the Gaumont Company, an arrangement that was, perhaps, not wholly satisfactory, for a year later Méliès transferred his favours to Pathé.

Méliès was immersed in the theatre again. In the spring of 1910 he mounted a pantomime, *The Phantoms of the Nile*, at the Paris Alhambra and then the Olympia. Later the revue went on tour to Grenoble, Louvain, Madrid, the Balearic Islands, Oran and Algeria, an impresario called Jos Hasting handling the publicity for this production.

Meanwhile, the Méliès Manufacturing Company in the U.S.A. had obtained a licence from the M.P.P.C. to produce a reel of film a week which would alternate with Georges' contribution and take the pressure off the Paris studios where all was far from well. In 1909 Gaston and Paul Méliès moved from Chicago to Fort Lee, near New York, which was at that time the capital of the Franco–American film industry. Pathé and Éclair had studios there. *The Stolen Wireless* was the company's first production, realised a year after its formation, and released on October 13 1909. It was a 15-minute war-drama "that held the interest of the spectators with its scenery and action, in spite of the fact that the plot was difficult to follow".[39] Gaston Méliès seems to have

---

* "Méliès' pictures usually run to the trick and spectacular style, with an occasional effort at comedy. Photographic quality of Méliès' films is invariably good, but the comedy has not often been of a character to find appreciation among the American patrons of picture houses." (*New York Dramatic Mirror*, November 14 1908).

La Reproduction
de nos Clichés
est rigoureusement
INTERDITE

Développement
des Negatifs & Positifs
A FAÇON

Prix Modérés

Letter of September 27 1910, from P. Tainguy (for G. Méliès) to Léon Gaumont.

successfully organised a scenario competition. At the time this was a common method of securing material.

Early in 1910 the company was transferred to San Antonio, Texas, 100 miles from the Mexican border, where a Star Film Ranch was built and used as a studio. Mostly westerns were made there, some on a grand scale: for instance, three hundred extras, cadets from Southwestern Military Academy, were used for the battle scenes in *The Immortal Alamo*. The surrounding countryside afforded excellent locations and the Hot Wells Hotel often served as field headquarters. An advertisement in *The Moving Picture World* claimed that

The Méliès Manufacturing Company with their new equipment are producing a series of western pictures unsurpassed in detail and scenery. There is a reason: In the southern part of Texas and on the Mexican border their stock company of actors, especially selected for these

Gaston Méliès as the padre in *The Immortal Alamo* (1911).

plays, are doing the work right in the open with all the natural settings and local characters at their command . . . People may have seen moving pictures of the 'Wild West' taken in 'Hohokus' [New Jersey] or some other irrelevant place and they haven't seen the wild West at all. If you want to show them the real, genuine article of the wild and woolly; the native cowboy and rancheros, with chaperajos, sombreros and lariat; wild Indians in war paint and feathers, wait for these two 'record busters' from Texas: *Cyclone Pete in Matrimony* and *Branding the Thief*.[40]

Many of the cowboys in these pictures had worked in the Buffalo Bill Show and were fine horsemen. The company personnel also included William Haddock (manager-cum-producer), director Francis Ford (brother of John Ford), and cameraman William Paley. Francis and Edith Storey, chaperoned by their mother, were the leading players, together with William Clifford, Mildred Bracken, Jesse Gulledge and Anne Nichols. A young Daniel Reulos, son of Lucien Reulos, the ex-partner of Georges Méliès and, since Gaston's remarriage in 1907, the latter's brother-in-law, played the lead in *The Cowboy Kid*. Gaston Méliès often appeared in minor roles.

Publicity material for *An Unwilling Cowboy* (1911).

The Western Studio, Santa Paula, California (1911–12).

Back lot of the Western Studio. Daniel Reulos in the saddle.

By May 1911 American Wildwest, as the company was now called, moved lock, stock and barrel to Sulphur Mountain Springs, Ventura County, California, which was really nothing more than an encampment. A month later Gaston set up headquarters in Santa Paula, at the Western Studio. By this time the company, whose trademark was a horse's head in a horseshoe, was producing 1½ reels a week and Gaston Méliès was supplying the whole Star Film quota for the M.P.P.C.: brother Georges had all but ceased production in Paris. As only 300 metres were submitted weekly to the trust, the company always had 150 metres of film in reserve. Over 130 films were made between spring 1910 and summer 1912. Of this period William Haddock wrote:

It was a happy time, all right, but only when I could keep old man Méliès tame—which was some job . . . In those

G. Méliès
Star Films.
MARY'S STRATAGEM—No. 2.
Mary goes for a row upon the river and is captured by hostile Indians.

Edith Storey in *Mary's Stratagem* (1911?).

Daniel Reulos in the title-role of *The Cowboy Kid* (1912).

An unidentified film from the Gaston Méliès company.

days, prints were sold on 'standing' orders—that is, orders from the exchanges to the manufacturer. They had to order two weeks ahead, figuring that the sale of twenty prints got cost-of-film back. When I started with Méliès, his longest order had been between twenty-five and thirty prints. When I left him, his standing orders were between ninety and one hundred—and he had signed a contract with the Vitagraph Company, according to which, after he got through with the negatives in this country, they were able to buy the foreign rights. He was guaranteed one hundred prints of every picture and paid two cents a foot for every foot of film they used. Now you know, that was a sweet reward.[41]

In the summer of 1912 Gaston Méliès made up his mind to go on a tour of the South Seas and Asia to make documentaries with an exotic ambiance. Accordingly, he departed on July 24 with a party of twenty-two including his wife, scriptwriter Edmund Mitchell and his wife, a cameraman named Bracken (a relative of Mildred Bracken?), actress Irene Tracy and 'Johnny the Cowboy'. They sailed from San Francisco on *The Manuka*, bound for Tahiti, and by chance they embarked with that island's Governor, Giraud, with whom the Méliès party became friendly. On board ship Gaston filmed a comedy, *The Misfortunes of Mr and Mrs Mott on Their Trip to Tahiti*. Arriving in Papeete in late August he made a series of narrative films. Letters to Paul Méliès, who had remained in New York to distribute his father's films, complained that there was a lack of comfortable hotels and that the Tahitians were too civilised to be suitable for ethnographic films. Gaston also reported that the local people were mad about cowboys, to the extent that they had taken to wearing stetsons and bandanas. Boarding the yacht *La Zélée*, lent by the Governor, Gaston sailed to Bora Bora where he filmed native fishermen at work. In September the troupe left for New Zealand by way of Rarotonga, where it rained all the time. The company had problems. Bracken was always drunk and 'Johnny the Cowboy' was in hospital suffering from syphilis. Gaston then set sail for Singapore, and stopped off to film in Australia, Java and Cambodia. *The Yellow Slave*, a romance in which two lovers commit suicide by walking into the sea, the pockets of their kimonos stuffed with stones, was made in Yokohama, Japan, where documentaries about temple architecture and jiu-jitsu were also filmed.

This is probably a snapshot of Bracken, the drunken cameraman, posed with an actress from *A Cambodian Idyll* or *The Robber of Angkor* (1913).

Gaston Méliès in Angkor, with the cast of *Javanese Dancers* (1913).

A simple stage erected for the filming, in Yokohama, of *The Yellow Slave* (?). Gaston Méliès, in bowler-hat, sits beside the camera, on the side of which his company's trade-mark, a horse's head in an inverted horseshoe, can be seen (1913).

Ferdinand Zecca at left
and Charles Pathé.

Gaston's films were dispatched to Paul Méliès in New York, where they arrived not always in prime condition. The developing facilities *en route* had been primitive: in Australia, for example, there had been no water in which to wash the developed stock. Gaston intended to return to Europe via the Trans-Siberian Railway, filming along the way, but mortified by his son's accounts of the failure of his films (those that could be salvaged) and by his own poor physical condition (he was, after all, seventy years old), Gaston cut short his expedition and set out for Paris from Yokohama in May 1913. He sent instructions to his son to liquidate the company, which was sold to Vitagraph. Paul Méliès remained in the U.S.A. to distribute Gaumont films. In April 1914 Gaston was in Algeria. A year later, poisoned by shellfish, he died in Corsica. His estate amounted to $20,086.36.

In autumn 1911 Georges Méliès signed a contract with Charles Pathé, who undertook to finance and distribute Star Films on a profit-sharing basis with their maker. When this system of finance proved too risky for Pathé, who had his shareholders to consider, he made Méliès a personal loan instead, against the security of the Montreuil studios and villa. Pathé was to have first refusal on any new films, together with the right to trim them down to suit his requirements. In early September Méliès resumed film-making. During the last few months of 1911 he produced two films, *Les Hallucinations du Baron de Münchausen* and *Le Vitrail diabolique.*

The lack of success of these films, which Méliès blamed on

Cinderella, or the Glass
Slipper (1912). Cinderella
dreams of the prince: the
wall collapses to reveal
him (frame enlargement).

his obsolete cameras,[42] prompted Pathé to exercise his right to edit subsequent Star Films himself. He appointed Ferdinand Zecca to do this. Zecca, it has been claimed (by Méliès' embittered widow), was afraid that Méliès might replace him as Pathé's right-hand man, so he butchered, through ill-will or incompetence, the films that came within his reach. *Cinderella, or The Glass Slipper* suffered particularly badly and was cut from 54 to 33 minutes.* Alice Guy, who made most of Gaumont's pre-1905 films, tells the story of Zecca, briefly out of favour with Pathé in 1904, reduced to selling soap from door to door. One detail in particular moved her: "Zecca was wetting the soap to make it weigh more".[43]

Cinderella, or the Glass
Slipper (1912). Louise
Lagrange as Cinderella in
an alfresco shot (frame
enlargement).

During 1912, the final year of his cinematic career, Méliès produced four films. In *The Conquest of the Pole*, the Giant of the Snows, a huge marionette, devours and regurgitates a group of explorers who subsequently find themselves attracted by and stuck to the magnetic pole, an idea that had been used in Verne's story *The Sphinx of the Ice-fields* (1897).

* Nevertheless *Cinderella* contains some fine things. Most of it was shot out of doors, a practice common with Méliès at this period, using deep-focus photography and a camera that pans occasionally. The sequence 'Return Before Midnight' is tinted deep-blue. One scene is particularly startling: Cinderella is dreaming of her prince; her thoughts are made evident because the wall behind her *collapses* to reveal another deep set in which the prince is holding court. Her thoughts of him deviate, presumably, for the wall is reconstituted, using reverse motion. The nearest parallel to this device is the 'thinks' bubble of the comic strip.

The Conquest of the Pole (1912). Drawing by Méliès of the machinery used to animate the puppet 'Giant of the Pole'.

The curtailed *Cinderella, or The Glass Slipper* featured sixteen-year-old Louise Lagrange. When an irate and humiliated Méliès complained of the treatment his films had received at the hands of Zecca, Pathé promised it would not happen again. Nevertheless *Le Chevalier des neiges*, a fairy story, and *Le Voyage de la famille Bourrichon*, Méliès' last film, probably made at the end of 1912 and adapted from a music-hall production by Eugène Labiche, were similarly treated.

These films were unsuccessful. Georges Méliès had become an anachronism, an artist left behind by economic and aesthetic developments. Between April 1896 and December 1912 he had made 502 pictures,* each year producing an average of 99 minutes of film. Every week Méliès worked solidly to complete just under two minutes worth. During the exceptional year of 1908, toiling under extreme pressure, he turned out eleven minutes of film weekly.

Early in 1913 Méliès finally split with Pathé, who asked for his money back. As Méliès couldn't pay, his property at Montreuil passed over to his creditors. As it happened, the outbreak of the First World War obliged the government to declare a moratorium, and Méliès was able to hang on to his property until 1923.

During the first stages of the war, the Robert-Houdin, like all the other theatres in Paris, was closed down by the authorities. Nine months later it reopened to empty houses. Méliès was forced to let the building, which became a

* This figure does not include ten (?) untitled advertising films made between 1896 and 1900.

cinema, the Ciné-Salon, later renamed the Ciné-Actualités. In March 1914 he attempted to raise some cash by selling ten automata to Maskelyne in England, but the deal fell through. To add to Méliès' problems his wife Eugénie had died on May 3 1913.

In 1915 the Rue Galliéni studio was converted, firstly into a cinema for hospitalised soldiers, and then in 1917 into a theatre, the Théâtre des Variétés–Artistiques, which was run until its closure in 1923 by Méliès' daughter, Georgette. It was largely a family affair: Georgette, a soprano; Méliès himself, who designed sets, wrote revues and songs, performed as a second tenor and "took over 98 roles";[44] André Méliès, first comic; André's wife, a singer at the Opéra-Comique whose stage-name was Raymonde Matho; and Pierre Armand-Fix, Georgette's baritone husband; these appeared in productions of *Paul and Virginia*, *Tosca* and *Faust*. A typical programme, that of July 23–24 1921, announces firstly, *The Amateur Singer*, an operetta by M. Fix; secondly, *The Indian Trunk*, a trick presented by M. Méliès and performed by the Indian Delhi; thirdly, *The Resurrection of Cleopatra*, an illusion, with Mlle Renée; and fourthly, *Jeanette's Wedding*, a comic-opera by Victor Massé. Other rôles at the variety theatre were taken by Mmes Alice Tissot, Marbeau, de l'Odéon, Louise Lagrange, Françoise Rosay, Charlotte Blet, and Messieurs Maljournal, David and Henri Jeanson.

In 1917 Méliès' premises in the Passage de l'Opéra were requisitioned by the Army. The 400 films found in the ex-bootmaker's offices were melted down, on the orders of the receiver, to a chemical used in the production of shoe-heels. During the war Méliès performed for patients at a local military hospital. At this time he was composing jingoistic verses, monologues to be recited at his variety theatre: " . . . The Future? It is at hand, and soon revenge / *Slow*, mark you, but *sure*, will be taken on that breed / Which meets with the disgust of the human race / Fearsome, the pitiless hand looms large / And already makes the guilty tremble!"[45]

After August 1920 the Boulevard de l'Hôtel de Ville studio at Montreuil was occupied by a group of White Russian émigré film-makers, led by Joseph Yermoliev, Pathé's representative in Russia until 1917, then by Alexander Kamenka. In April 1920 the Chambre Syndicale de la Prestidigitation had begun to meet again, with Méliès presiding. On June 13 1920, Méliès gave the last show at the

Théâtre Robert-Houdin. Three years later the building was demolished to make way for the Boulevard Haussmann. Méliès stated in 1928 that he lost 460.000F when the Robert-Houdin was expropriated by the civil authorities, who reimbursed him with one year's rent—35.000F. To make matters worse, when he bought the theatre in 1888 from Mme Émile Robert-Houdin she had reserved the right to two-thirds of the indemnity of expropriation, a right that was claimed thirty-five years later.

In 1923 Méliès was being hounded by creditors. He was able to pay his debts by selling his property at Montreuil. It was a sad moment when the Méliès family had to leave. The vast property was chopped into bits and auctioned. Mme Nicolodi, who bought the lot with the variety theatre on it, permitted Méliès and his daughter to stay in the flat above where, shortly afterwards, a granddaughter was born. Méliès' stock of prints was sold by the kilo to a dealer in second-hand films in the Rue Bergère. In a moment of despair Méliès personally destroyed a batch of negatives. During the summer of 1923 the Montreuil troupe, still intact, were on tour near Tréport, on the Channel. In the spring of 1924 Méliès was proud to announce to his colleagues in the conjuring union the success of their annual fête: the tombola had made 91F profit! During the summer Méliès joined his daughter Georgette on tour at Sables-d'Olonne. A few weeks later he was commissioned, with André Méliès, by the Mines de la Sarre to reconstitute the machinery of a Saarbrücken theatre, destroyed by the retreating Germans. This work took up the autumn months.

By 1925 the Méliès family had broken up, for the loan period on the Montreuil flat had expired. Georgette went to live with her in-laws, André with his. The most sensible thing for Méliès to do was remarry. His ex-mistress Jehanne d'Alcy, née Charlotte-Stéphanie Faes, known as Fanny Manieux, became the old man's second wife on December 10 1925. A few years previously Jehanne d'Alcy had bought a small shop, selling chocolates, sweets and toys (trumpets, pop-guns, wheelbarrows, dolls and yoyos) on the street outside the Gare Montparnasse. Later on, the business shifted into the station concourse, into the Salle des Pas Perdus. Méliès and his wife, herself a widow, lived in a tiny apartment near by, on the Square Jolivet. An announcement of their marriage appeared in the December 18 edition of *Ciné-Journal*, proof that Méliès had not been entirely forgotten. Life was none the less difficult:

This was perhaps the most arduous part of his life, for the shop had to be open from 7 in the morning until 10 at night. It was impossible to leave it, even for a meal; no Sunday, no evening was free. It was a prison for a man who had been used to total freedom. Running this shop, in a court exposed to draughts, glacial in winter, torrid in summer, was murder for an already very old man.[46]

On June 23 1926, Méliès heard by letter that he had been made first honorary member of the Chambre Syndicale Française de la Cinématographie. From August 6 to September 17 he published a series of articles, *En marge de l'histoire de Cinématographe*, in *Ciné-Journal* (nos. 884–90). The magazine's editor was Léon Druhot, the person who, according to an apocryphal story told by Méliès, discovered the old man completely by chance selling sweets and toys in his little shop in the Gare Montparnasse. In the September 24 edition of his magazine Druhot drew his readers' attention to Méliès' precarious material situation.

In 1929 a cache of Star Films was found by J.-P. Mauclaire, the director of Studio 28, an avant-garde ciné-club, in the dairy of a large house belonging to Jean Rives, the executor of the will of M. Dufayel, a wealthy furniture seller who had shown them in 1900 in the publicity cinema of his shop on the Boulevard Barbès. A dozen tinted films were recovered, their perforations ruined. New prints were made and coloured. On December 16 a Méliès Gala, organised by Paul Gilson and J.-G. Auriol, under the patronage of two newspapers owned by the perfumier Coty, was held at the Salle Pleyel. A big crowd turned out to see eight Star Films, together with *The Cheat* (1915) by Cecil B. De Mille and a short, made for the occasion by Gilson, of Méliès making a spectacular entrance on stage.

Cover of the programme of the Gala Méliès.

During 1929 Méliès had presented his collection of Robert-Houdin's automata to the Conservatoire National des Arts et Métiers. On enquiring four years later why the machines were not on display the old man was told that the automata had been destroyed by a beam falling during the modification of the warehouse that contained them. This was a lie: Landais, the curator of the museum, had resold the lot.

In June 1930 the Group l'Éffort announced an evening of Méliès films, or 'filmlets', as the magazine *Close Up* called them. On October 21 1931, Méliès was awarded the Cross of the Legion of Honour. "A superb evening," Méliès beamed in a letter to Gilson, "with rousing speeches and non-stop cheering."[47] Unfortunately his material situation had not improved. There was talk, though, of a trip to Hollywood to make films.

After years of neglect the original studio was in a sorry state. Most of the glass panes were broken, vegetation had sprung up inside, and to avoid accidents the trapdoors had been filled in. In one of the dressing-rooms a list of props was still visible: the fantastic egg, costumes for the devils, magic balls. Backcloths designed by Méliès were to be found in a corner under a pile of planks, broken chairs and old mattresses. The studio was used to store junk. It was finally demolished after the war.

In September 1932 Méliès, his wife and granddaughter Madeleine, whose mother had died in 1930 after a long illness contracted in Algeria while on tour there, were given an apartment in a château at Orly, near Paris, run by the Mutuelle du Cinéma. The old couple were finding life harder than they had expected: they had no maid nor cook and their benefactors' agent, an ex-policeman called Guyollot, kept a tight financial rein on them. Méliès spent his time drawing and writing letters, many of them to curious film historians. In a letter to the Chambre Syndicale de la Prestidigitation he announced that he was ready to resign, for apart from his dissatisfaction at the union's gradual dissolution, he found the cost of travelling from Orly to Paris too high for his meagre resources. The union members agreed to defray this cost from their petty cash fund. In 1932 there was a project afoot to film *The Phantom of the Métro*

Méliès appearing in a publicity short for La Régie des Tabacs (1935).

with Méliès as technical advisor, to be directed by Marcel Carné and scripted by the Prévert brothers. On March 15 1934, Méliès, complaining of ill-health (he had been confined to bed for six months), resigned as president of the Chambre Syndicale de la Prestidigitation and became its honorary president instead.

During 1935 he participated with Jacques Prévert, Paul Grimault and Jean Aurenche as an actor on two publicity shorts for La Régie des Tabacs. He wrote scripts for more films like these, but none were made. At the time of his death he was about to contribute to a new version of *Baron Münchausen* (his own dates from 1911), to be directed by the dadaist film-maker, Hans Richter. The latter had been introduced to Méliès by Henri Langlois, who had shown the old man a number of Richter's experimental films. The abstract ones had left Méliès bemused; the trick ones, like *Ghosts Before Breakfast* (1927–8), had fired his imagination. The project was shelved when Richter left for Switzerland to make commercial films.

And then, on January 21 1938, after an illness lasting three months, Georges Méliès, aged seventy-six, died of cancer at the Hôpital Léopold-Bellan in Paris. He was buried at Père Lâchaise cemetery on the 25th.

Funeral service for Georges Méliès (January 25 1938).

Méliès' grave. The bust was added in 1954.

Star Film Critique

"Subjects dependent on the imagination are infinitely varied and inexhaustible."—Georges Méliès

A Protean World

A romanesque chamber that is obviously a treasury forms the setting of *The Treasures of Satan*, a two-and-threequarter-minute comedy made in 1902. The chamber is a painted backcloth. To the left is a fireplace, next to that a window. The central area is occupied by a passageway the floor of which slopes away against all the laws of perspective.* The gloomy tunnel contains a number of chests and moneybags. To the right of it are a chair and chest surmounted by two skulls and more sacks of gold. The real furniture in this sombre setting consists of three stools, a chest, and a table which has half a dozen moneybags on it, each one marked '50000'. Satan, sporting a pointed beard, cloak, doublet, tights and twin-feathered cap (his horns), enters and surveys the scene. He hails two henchmen, dressed in sixteenth-century costume. They bring forward a chest, $7' \times 3' \times 3'$, show it to be empty and place it across two stools. Then, forming a chain with their master, they proceed to toss the bags of gold to each other before putting them in the chest. The two accomplices leave Satan to check on the chest's security. Satan, carrying a huge key, exits left. From the right a knavish character crawls into view. It is Georges Méliès, dressed in tights, pointed hat, blonde wig and beard. With a dagger he prises open the chest lid, but it descends on his fingers. After he has extricated them he lifts the lid, only to be surprised by the six moneybags which have assumed a life of their own. He closes the lid and sits on it, but is tossed off when the lid rises to disclose a pretty girl wearing a more demure version of Satan's costume. She leaps to the ground and is then followed by five friends, much to the consternation of the thief. The girls line up behind the chest, each one holding a bag of gold aloft which changes into a spear with a fearsome point. They chase the thief who jumps into the chest

---

* Méliès, like de Chirico and Uccello, was aware that distortions in linear perspective can suggest malaise and mystery. When he paints a vista on a backcloth the confusion between real space (actual objects painted to blend with their setting) and that artificial space adds a further metaphysical dimension to the image.

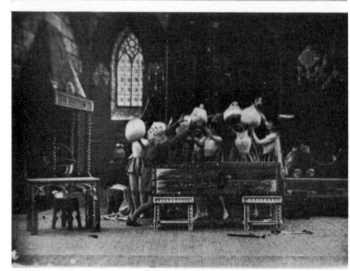

The Treasures of Satan
(1902). Méliès at left
(frame enlargement).

Bags of gold turn into
spears in *The Treasures of
Satan* (1902). (Consecu-
tive frame enlargements).

which disappears leaving him exposed to their assault. The same thing happens when he seeks refuge in an upright chest. He hides his face and his attackers disappear. Suddenly the horizontal chest, which reappeared soon after it disappeared, stands up of its own accord. The thief hits it with a stool and it is replaced by a white-clad acrobat who proceeds to turn a few somersaults before chasing the thief. The horizontal chest, which has appeared again, is open and Méliès tumbles into it. No sooner is he inside when smoke begins to pour out of it, followed by enormous flames. All Satan's agents reappear and perform a victory jig. The chest explodes. All that remains are six bags of swag.

A bag of gold becomes a spear; a wooden chest changes into an acrobat. Méliès' aesthetic consists of periodical dislocations, of spectacular, metamorphic images supported by subservient ones, of lawless unpredictable pantomime. The ideal forms to cope with this frantic dialectic are conjuring tricks, dreams, odysseys and fairy stories. His marvellous world is one of objects in flux, of objects that find it impossible to retain their identity (and because humans are treated as objects too, there is just a hint of madness, of schizophrenia, behind Méliès' genial exterior).

An object can be transformed either instantaneously or gradually into another object; an object can grow or diminish before our eyes, while the rest of the image remains a constant size; an object, usually human, can disintegrate into its parts, then these can assume a life of their own; an inanimate object can begin to move and an animate one to defy the laws of gravity; and an object can appear or disappear instantaneously or gradually.

Human beings are treated as objects, as *puppets*. Méliès the puppeteer in *Punch and Judy* (1906).

Méliès had his favourite, protean images: participants in a game whose driving force is the denial of expectancy and the exploitation of the dynamic instant between the anxiety of dislocation and its release in the ensuing humorous or dreamlike image.

The statue that comes to life is such an elected image. Not only statues, but scarecrows, snowmen, dummies, skeletons, figures in paintings, posters, photographs, playing cards and book illustrations, pulsate with life, through the camera's stop–motion capability. In *The Adventures of William Tell* (1898) a clown trying to emulate the yeoman's feat places a cabbage on the helmet of a suit of armour, which becomes animated and assaults the unfortunate archer. Watched over by a conjuror who has a moving marble statue for an assistant four diminutive kings and queens, exiles from a pack of cards, dance *The Lilliputian Minuet* (1905). In *Punch and Judy* (1906) the marionettes become human and attack the puppeteer. Méliès had constructed during the 1880s replicas of Robert-Houdin's mechanical figures, figures which 'came to life'.

Transformations often take place in a well, vase or font. 'Water as a magical element' is an image common enough in fairy tales. 'Plunging into a lake to meet a fairy' or 'the appearance of a guardian spirit near a grotto or spring' are two of the commonest. In *The Enchanted Well* (1903) a peasant suffers the misfortune of having his well cursed by a witch. When he attempts to draw water he gets fire instead. The well swells to form a tower from which

Maskelyne's attempt to bring a painting to life, *The Artist's Dream*, an illusion invented by David Devant in 1893. A picture comes to life in *A Spiritualistic Photographer* (1903).

monstrous creatures emerge. In the end the peasant is flung down the well by huge frogs.

Images of the traveller who can find no rest and the diner who can never eat his food are common. When a weary traveller puts up at an inn he must expect to be tormented by a moving candle that grows, explodes or goes out, by boots that walk by themselves, by a dancing bed or pyrotechnic furniture, a huge bedbug, mischievous goblin or ghastly dummy animated by practical jokers. When a diner sits down to eat he must expect the table legs to grow, the table and everything on it to disappear, run away, catch fire or explode. An hotel dining-room is demolished on more than one occasion by a rampaging automobile.

It was Lewis Carroll who, like Méliès, employed the image of the frustrated diner with humorous effect, and the following joke of his predicts both the technique (running a film backwards) and ironic type of humour the cinema's earliest audiences found irresistible: "An empty fork is raised to the lips: there it receives a neatly-cut piece of mutton, and swiftly conveys it to the mutton already there. Soon one of the plates, furnished with a complete slice of mutton and two potatoes, was handed up to the presiding gentleman, who quietly replaced the slice on the joint, and the potatoes in the dish."[1]

Humour was essential and natural to the primitive cinema; its language was, after all, largely restricted to the exploitation of technical trickery, and its audience was to be found seeking *amusement* in fairgrounds and variety theatres. Just

Confusion at *The Inn Where No Man Rests* (1903).

A delirious dinner in *The Merry Frolics of Satan* (1906). Scene 17, 'The Demonic Soirée in the Kitchen'.

A poem by Méliès, *La Sêmeuse* (1916).

about all of Méliès' five-hundred-odd films are comedies. Joking is a dynamic part of the unstable, protean world of Star Film. When we witness objects liberated from the external regulations that bind them, our internal inhibitions go by the board as well: sources of pleasure, rendered inaccessible by these inhibitions, are made accessible. We, too, feel liberated and amused. Although Méliès occasionally indulged in satire, his favourite kind of humour was the practical joke. It is ironical that Méliès made his comedies—"staggering salvoes of comic go-getting", they were called[2]—with actors dressed in a funeral grey and wearing grey make-up dancing through mournful sets painted in grisaille, a precaution taken because of the eccentric film stock then used.

It was another poet who first recognised Méliès' poetic cinema. Apollinaire said: "M. Méliès and I are in the same business. We lend enchantment to vulgar material." Yet Méliès was surprised to find himself thus acclaimed, and he expressed his confusion in a letter to Paul Gilson. Written in 1937, it shows quite clearly his naïve conception of poetry:

I have written verses, just like everyone else. I've made up songs that were sung at the Robert-Houdin during the war. I've concocted a three-act revue enacted at the Théâtre Le Peletier and five or six comedies performed with success at my variety theatre at Montreuil. But this scant literary baggage would never authorise me to figure honourably beside any celebrated man of letters.[3]

In his automatic writings Benjamin Péret, the French surrealist, created a playful and irreverent world which is close in spirit to Méliès' own. Péret's irrational images evolve in a profusion of subordinate clauses. We might cite, for comparison, Péret's tomato that danced with an artichoke, the horse that played hide-and-seek with its cab, and the deaf men who put their ears out to dry on piano wires. It's *The Melomaniac* once again!

The Melomaniac (1903).

The set for *Extraordinary Illusions* (1903, one and a-half minutes long) is a stage. Three-quarters of the picture-plane consists of a rear wall covered with wallpaper, mouldings, paintings and candelabra, in front of which stand several plinths with statues and a vase on them. The wall is pierced by a doorway the lintel of which bears the words, 'foyer de la danse' ('Dancers' Green Room'). The portal, situated off-centre, encloses a shadowy space with just a suggestion of hanging curtains. The whole surface is two-dimensional, painted in *trompe-l'œil*, with sunlight falling from right to left. Before the dark doorway stands a small table.

It is on this table that a seated Chinaman, a parasol in his left hand, a fan in his right, slowly materialises. Getting down from the table he takes a turn around the stage before remounting it. He leaps into space and the moment his feet touch the ground he changes into a conjuror, Méliès himself. Méliès is wearing the costume he has favoured since 1885: a short jacket, knee breeches and silk stockings, as well as a *toupee*, for he had become bald in his twenties. Throughout the film Méliès the showman moves with suppleness and grace, making expressive gestures with his hands to emphasise actions and effects, and pointing his toes as he struts about the stage. After bowing to the audience he orders the table to do a couple of somersaults, which it does. Making use of the wings off-camera to deposit and acquire props the conjuror swaps the parasol he has borrowed from the vanished Chinaman for a shallow, rectangular box. He points out the words on its lid: 'Magical Box' it says, in English this time. Showing the box to be empty, he puts it on the table, coaxes the lid open from a distance, and removes a long, white sheet from it. Going to the edge of the stage he lifts a simple wooden stand into view. From the box he draws a pair of legs, then a dummy's torso and finally a head. As the box is so shallow Méliès uses stop-motion to make these bulky objects appear to come from inside it. The box is tossed to the floor and commanded to quit the scene. Bringing the dummy to the foreground the conjuror kisses it before tossing it gently into the air. As it lands the dummy is transformed into a ballerina. He changes her tutu for two other sets of clothes, one scantier (a maillot and sash), the other more demure (an ankle-length dress). The conjuror gives the girl a piggy-back to the table and sits her on it, at which point she changes into a chef madly stirring the contents of a saucepan. Méliès is appalled. He leaps on to the table and kicks the chef's backside, turning him into the pretty girl he was. Next she is tied up in a large cloth. The whole bundle explodes, showering the stage with bits of paper that fall like snow. As these fragments settle we see the wholesome lady standing on the table. Méliès goes to help her down but to his chagrin she turns into the chef once again. The conjuror can stand no more: he literally rips the man to pieces, leaps on to the table and gradually vanishes, leaving the stage as deserted as it was to begin with.

It is perfectly natural that a superior optical illusion like the cinema should find itself initially in the hands of conjurors, who are often expert mechanics, and are well acquainted with optical trickery, such as mirror masking, reflected images, transparent reflections, lantern projection, background work and chiaroscuro.[4] (In mirror masking the legs of a table hide the edges of a mirror behind which a person is concealed. Mirrors are used to make an object appear where none exists, in the reflected image. Transparent reflections utilise an image projected on to a sheet of glass. Lantern projections speak for themselves. Background work entails masking by means of a screen having the same colour as a background. Painting a flat surface to represent a concave or convex one, or disguising a hollow or projection to resemble a plain surface, is a feature of chiaroscuro.) Frenchmen like Claude Grivolas, Émile and Vincent Isola, Félicien Trewey, Gaston Velle and Méliès were both conjurors and film-makers; as were Nevil Maskelyne, David Devant and Walter R. Booth* in England and Leopoldo Fregoli in Italy.

* Walter R. Booth's cinematic career is an interesting one. Beginning as a conjuror, he went on to direct trick films for R. W. Paul (1896–1906), the Urban Trading Company (for which he made the first British animated cartoon, *The Hand of the Artist*, in April 1906), and Kineto (1911), colour films for Urban's Natural Colour Kinematograph Company (1912), and sound films for U.K. Kineplastikon Films (1913).

Méliès used the camera to rejuvenate conjuring, to link single illusions in a delirious sequence limited only by the length of the film-strip. In condensing his spectacular illusions he was able to intensify the magical experience.

In one sense the early cinema turned to the marvellous because it had to take its place in a marvellous context. Méliès' work must be situated amidst other entertainments to be found in the magic theatres, fairground booths, wax museums and café-concerts with which films first vied.

Lentiélectroplasticromomimocoliserpentographe was the name José Fessi Fernandez, a famous entrepreneur, gave to his fairground cinema. His fellow showmen used other means to attract their customers. Dancers, clowns, acrobats, jugglers, contortionists and trapeze artistes were employed to gain the attention of the passing crowds. The *Cinématographe* had appeared at a fair in Saint-Nazaire in September 1896 and was soon followed by a large number of imitations, including Méliès and Reulos' *Kinétograph*. Films were shown to the accompaniment of roaring lions, noisy traction engines, organ music and the hurly-burly of the crowds.

Waxworks were popular. Large tableaux like *The Last Moments of the Illustrious Poet Victor Hugo*, *Gorilla Seizing a Young Girl* and a mechanical *Raft of the Medusa* could be seen, and *actualités* encapsulating news events: portraits of Dreyfus; the Czar on his death-bed; and Vidal, the murderer of women. Theatres of *tableaux vivants* stood side by side with puppet theatres that presented shows like *A Trip to the Moon*. Next door to menageries would be anatomical museums full of morbid exhibits and scientific curiosities: the corpse of a man who had died from hunger, a drowned woman, preserved crocodiles and octopi, and a back room, full of freaks, strictly reserved for gentlemen. One showman, who claimed to be a defrocked priest, exhibited "the child-Voltaire's skull",[5] an invention worthy of Raymond Roussel.

Fairground publicity: wrestlers, dancers, clowns and a man with a revolver.

A fairground menagerie.

A serpentine dancer stands behind the seated owner of this fairground *Bioscope* show.

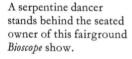

A brown bear with its head shorn of fur became 'The Pig-Faced Lady'. Shoals of trained goldfish, secured to toy boats by fine wires, enacted naval engagements, and oysters smoked pipes. 'Glass Tank Swimming Shows' were extremely popular: performers ate and drank under water, played cards and retrieved coins with their mouths. Magic lantern slides were projected on to the voluminous, bat-winged dress of a danseuse, while the 'woman-screen' performed a Serpentine Dance à la Loie Fuller.*

Meanwhile, in the city of Paris, in the vicinity of the Robert-Houdin, conjuring and film-shows, waxwork displays, palmistry and pantomimes could be enjoyed at a number of small theatres. At the café-concerts, crippled, hunchbacked and blind performers were particularly appreciated. Tattooed men and women, albinos, the armless and legless, giants, dwarfs, bearded ladies, skeletal and obese persons: it was side by side with human anomalies like these that Méliès' own 'mutations'—the man with the rubber head, the armless clown of *Dislocation Extraordinary*, the fat man of *Hydrothérapie fantastique*, the white-skinned negroes of *Off to Bloomingdale Asylum*, the tiny figures of *The Lilliputian*

* "The Count and Countess Pecci-Blunt gave an elaborate costume-ball in their house and garden in Paris. The theme was white; any costume was admitted but it had to be all in white. A large white dance floor was installed in the garden with the orchestra hidden in the bushes. I was asked to think up some added attraction. I hired a movie projector which was set up in a room on an upper floor, with the window giving out on the garden. I found an old hand-coloured film by the pioneer French film-maker, Méliès. While the white couples were revolving on the white floor, the film was projected on this moving screen—those who were not dancing looked down from the windows of the house. The effect was eerie." (Man Ray, *Self Portrait*, 1963).

Minuet, the enormous ones of *The Dwarf and the Giant*—appeared.

Méliès' substitutions are irrational and therefore perplexing. He called them "mystical". We would call them cryptic. It is interesting to note that the substitution cipher is an important device in cryptography (secret writing): one set of letters stands for another. In an advertising film he made to sell chocolate Méliès used frame-by-frame animation to shuffle a jumble of letters into the recognisable brand name, *Meunier*. When he changed one object into another he also changed its name: to do so was to grant it semantic freedom. Of her grandfather Madeleine Malthête-Méliès said: "He liked jokes with words."[6]

For Ado Kyrou this process of transmutation leads naturally to the analogy of the cinema with alchemy: Méliès' "work and his life, his films and his dreams, the dreams in his films and the life of his dreams, pass through the retort that is the camera to emerge unified, the philosopher's stone of the cinema."[7] According to Chaplin*, Méliès was "a

The laboratory/workshop: the world of men for Méliès. Scene 2 of *The Merry Frolics of Satan* (1906).

* Strangely enough Méliès detested Chaplin's type of humour.

veritable alchemist of light".[8] Many a Star Film setting contains alchemical accessories: flasks, *memento mori*, furnaces, retorts and dusty tomes. If, as we shall see, a woman's place is to be in the midst of flowers, shells and insects, the laboratory (and the factory) comprises the world of men for Méliès. And his alchemists are such mercenary scientists, completely lacking in the idealism of the real alchemist (whose search for the philosopher's stone was a symbolic, not pecuniary, one), that their experiments never end in anything but comedy (*The Philosopher's Stone*, 1899; *The Mysterious Retort*, 1906). It was the world of unattractive work, of work done solely for profit, that Méliès poked fun at.

Recalcitrant Heads, Arms, Legs

The Man With the Rubber Head (1902, two-and-threequarter minutes), is set in a laboratory—a sign above a window on the right says so. Painted on the wall is a thermometer, medicine chest and some shelves with retorts, bottles, globes and bowls on them. A pair of bellows is propped up in the corner. The rear wall bears a large doorway. It is before this black aperture that magical transformations will take place.

An apothecary (Georges Méliès) appears, in shirtsleeves and waistcoat, a felt hat on his head, cigarette in his mouth, and long, white apron just about covering him from top to toe. First of all he performs the cryptic operation of pouring liquid from one bottle into another one, which rests on a stool in the foreground. Moving the stool to one side and opening the large doors in the rear wall, he brings forward an ornate table to the front of the stage. On it he places a small stand which is fitted with a curved pipe and a stop-cock, the function of which he demonstrates in mime. From a small box a living head the duplicate of his own is produced and placed centrally on the stand. Méliès sits on a stool beside the table, takes off his hat and points out the similarity between his head and the other one, before going on to mime the idea of expansion. As he fetches the bellows from the corner of the lab the head on the stand begins to look apprehensive and shakes itself. The bellows are connected to the piping.* Méliès begins pumping and the head starts to grow larger, all the time gasping like a drowning man suffering from a lack, not a surfeit, of oxygen. It grows four feet high before the tap is turned off and then opened to let the 'rubber' head† down.

* Compressed air was used to animate some of Robert-Houdin's automata.

† Barnum and Bailey exhibited James Morris, whose epidermis was so elastic that he could cover his face with the distended skin of his chin and neck.

The Man With the Rubber Head (1902) (frame enlargements).

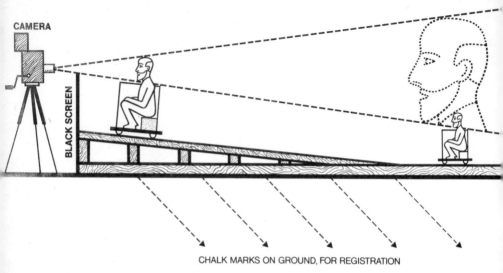

CAMERA

BLACK SCREEN

CHALK MARKS ON GROUND, FOR REGISTRATION

How Méliès' head grows in *The Man With the Rubber Head.*

When it is deflated the apothecary fetches his assistant, whose face is made up like a clown's. After being given a demonstration the assistant takes over. In a moment both the head and the apothecary are looking extremely concerned, with good reason, for the incompetent clown blows up the head to such an extent that it explodes in a great puff of smoke, sending both men and furniture flying. After throwing his assistant out of the window the apothecary, reduced to tears, sobs into his apron.

Méliès asks us to imagine two things: that a severed head can go on living and that several copies of such a unusual extremity can exist at the same time. The films themselves take two forms. A severed head simply appears, alive and well, such as on a pedestal (*Pygmalion and Galatea*, 1898), amid flames (*Alcofrisbas, the Master Magician*, 1903), or in a bubble (*Soap Bubbles*, 1906). Alternatively, an artiste—it's always Méliès—is able to reproduce as many as six severed heads exactly like his own, with various consequences. *Tit For Tat, or a Good Joke With My Head* (1904) is about one head assaulting another. A juggler blows smoke into the face of a head just like his own. The severed head revenges itself by squirting water on to its twin, and the juggler retaliates by forcing the floating head into a hat. In *The Four Troublesome Heads* (1898) a conjuror punishes three recalcitrant heads that sing out of tune by hitting them with a banjo, which makes them disappear. The fourth one—his own—he takes from his shoulders and throws into the air. It lands on his neck again. In *The King of the Sharpshooters* (1905) a rifleman provides a candelabrum with five duplicates of his head, four of which he proceeds to shoot away. His body is eventually reunited with the remaining head. "The marvel of the trick is that the sharpshooter is able to get a new head as soon as he parts with the old one."[9]

Sado-masochistic images like these have an unconscious vitality all of their own. They are retributive (under the auspices of humour the magician retaliates against replicas of himself) yet egotistic (he fabricates his duplicate, then destroys it to assert his uniqueness).

In conjuring the performer makes much of his ability to control mechanical men (Robert-Houdin and his automata) or even his own double (the Davenports and their lay figures). The seemingly free psychic flow from the human to the mechanical or artificial is at the heart of many illusions, although the performer's power is always of a more material nature (compressed air, electricity, clockwork; darkness and subterfuge). The conjuror's dialogue with mechanical man, and his complete control over him, underlines his uniqueness, his superiority over men rendered 'mechanical' by the nature of their work. In a stylised manner the conjuror, an artisan through and through, is able to assert his independence from capitalism and industrialism. The conjuror makes a mechanical man out of machinery, machinery does not make a mechanical man out of him.

Along with cups and balls and the knife through the arm the decapitation illusion is one of the oldest in the magician's bag. The Westcar Papyrus, written in 1700 B.C., describes the most famous feat of the conjuror Dedi of Dedsnefru: replacing the severed heads of geese, pelicans and oxen.[10] It is in shamanism that conjuring seems to have its origins. The shaman is the healer, mystic visionary, professional hysteric, and specialist in ecstasy. At his initiation the shaman often sees images of his own dismemberment in a dream; his head is cut off by demons, his profane body is in dissolution, and a new personality is born. Modern conjuring, with its images of dismemberment, might represent the degeneration of shamanism from profound mystical experience to didactic entertainment.

Méliès was one in a long line of magicians, which includes J. N. Maskelyne, who specialised in the decapitation illusion.* Heads take leave of bodies in five of Méliès' theatrical

* "They cut a man's head off—no matter / Though body and head be apart / The latter is seen to chatter / In a way to make nervous folks

illusions. In *The Fairy of the Flowers* (1889) a woman's head appears in a bouquet of flowers, in *The Enchanted Spring* (1892) floating in space. A knight's head ends up in the dial of a clock, in *The Up-to-Date Mountebank* (1892). *Alcofrisbas the Enchanter* (1889) is an early draft of *American Spiritualistic Mediums* (1891) and a parody of the Davenport Brothers school of conjuring. Alcofrisbas is a classical figure in the fairy-theatre, or *féerie*, and figured in many productions at the Châtelet. In the 1891 sketch a man's head is swapped for a skeleton's.

Comparison between the stage illusions and the films shows just how liberating the cinema was for Méliès. It enabled him to use the image of the living, severed head to even greater effect, for he saw how the photographic fidelity, duplication potential, and plastic qualities of film could make numerous disembodied heads appear.

The bizarre happenings in *Dislocation Extraordinary* (1901) unfold before the mouth of a cave hung with stalactites. On the stage before the painted backdrop is a seat, in fact a rectangular board painted to look like one, flanked by two stools, one supporting a bottle, the other a candle and glass.

A pierrot, in white costume and pointed hat decorated with pompoms, comes to the front of the stage, looks to the right and left to see that nobody is looking and proceeds to mime the act of sitting on the seat. He sits down and looks towards the bottle four feet away before miming the act of drinking. However, he can reach neither glass nor bottle from where he sits. Suddenly his right arm detaches itself, floats through the air, and returns grasping the bottle. His left arm follows suit in grabbing the glass. It is obvious that the scene has been shot against a black background using black garments to hide parts of the body, the whole being superimposed on the cavern setting. The clown drinks. His arms begin travelling again, to replace the bottle and glass. He calls them back; the objects reappear on the stools by themselves.

From his copious costume the pierrot produces a clay pipe. He wants to light it, so his head floats to the burning candle to accomplish this. Then his legs leave his body, take their place on the two stools and start to dance. Suddenly the seat disappears and the clown's torso tumbles to the ground. He calls for support

---

start / Till they find that fast on its shoulders / The head still continues to grow / Though how, bothers all the beholders / 'Twould puzzle a lawyer to know !" (*Barney Maguire's Account of his Visit to Maskelyne and Cooke's Entertainment*, 1877).

from his legs: they obey him. Intact once more he jumps for joy. But then each appendage leaves the pierrot's trunk, and twists and turns in mid-air before coming together once more. The clown takes off his head, sits on it then puts it back on his shoulders. The film ends when the pierrot, played, it is said, by André Deed, the acrobatic comedian who was to make a name for himself as (variously) Cretinetti, Gribouille, Glupishkin and Foolshead, comes forward and takes a bow.

Arms and legs also have a habit of leaving bodies in Star Film comedies. Occasionally the bits are wrongly assembled, as in *Up-to-Date Surgery* (1902), in which a patient, afflicted with indigestion, has his limbs and head amputated only to have them put back in the wrong order by a demented doctor, so that an arm ends up where a leg should be, and vice versa. In *Jack Jaggs and Dum Dum* (1903) a man's body and head are joined to a dancer's skirt and legs, a truly 'exquisite corpse'.* These films are full of the kind of black humour that makes one think of the sailor who sported the macabre tattoo, a dotted line encircling his neck, together with the legend 'cut here', or the character in one of Raymond Roussel's novels who made a flute from the tibia of his amputated leg.

The image of the severed limb (especially the hand) is emotionally disturbing. We might cite here the ethereal hands the Davenport Brothers caused to appear at their cabinet séances in the early 1860s, the severed hand with painted fingernails that figures in Dali and Buñuel's *Un Chien Andalou* (1928), and the malevolent *Beast With Five Fingers*, of Robert Florey's 1947 film.†

Méliès' editing is purely objective and, save for the occasional tracking shot, like the rocket's approach to the man-in-the-moon's eye in *A Trip to the Moon*, so is his camera. It is the imagery, rather than the structure, of his films that is emotionally charged. It may make them appear primitive to an audience conditioned to montage and camera movement, yet this 'weakness' is a strength—as Buñuel has never tired of repeating—as it permits the untrammelled expression and direct experience of the image. In Méliès' work the inflexibility and monotony of his style, with its static camera

* The 'exquisite corpse', or *cadavre exquis*, is a surrealist game in which a drawing is made by three or four people who are ignorant of one another's contribution.

† As a boy Florey used to attend shows at the Théâtre Robert-Houdin.

A severed hand appears in this satirical drawing by Méliès of a spirit medium.

The conjurer Harmington runs him through as Marius is accosted by a severed hand. These two artistes appeared regularly at the Robert-Houdin.

and relentless, pulsating form, coaxes the spectator into a euphoric state, a condition of reverie, the better to receive and respond to the images of disorientation that are the focal points of his work. As Bachelard has pointed out, reverie is a condition auspicious for the poetic experience.

Women

The action of *The Brahmin and the Butterfly*, a two-minute caution-ary tale made in 1900, unfolds before a backcloth upon which is painted a Rousseauesque tropical forest scene, not without a few anachronistic plants (pansies, cacti) among the vegetation (ferns, orchids, lianas). From the wings, formed of cutouts representing more foliage, a brahmin (Méliès) in a striped kaftan and turban appears. After suggesting its form by a movement of the hands, the brahmin fetches an egg-shaped cocoon and suspends it from wires. He produces a flute and plays it to such effect that a large caterpillar—not a snake—appears from the wings, crawls over to

*The Brahmin and the
Butterfly* (1900). (Consecutive frame enlargements).

the magician and lifts its head to whisper something in his ear. He kisses it and then places it in the cocoon. A moment later a butterfly-woman starts to emerge from the chrysalis and, aided by a wire of course, rises into the air where she flutters her wings, drying them. The brahmin takes the cocoon away. The butterfly-woman, whose striped bodice makes her look more like a wasp (another 'confusion'—is this a dream?), stands on the palm of his hand, descends to the ground and then begins to dance around the stage. In the meantime the hindu has produced a large striped cloth with which he pursues the fabulous insect, eventually catching and covering her with it. Two attendants in oriental costume appear and, as the brahmin congratulates himself, they remove the cloth: the butterfly-woman has changed into an eastern princess. The magician decides to court her. When he kneels to kiss her foot she puts it on his head and in an instant he is changed into the same caterpillar from which the marvellous insect evolved. Now the haughty princess and her attendants quit the scene and the disconsolate caterpillar, wishing it were a brahmin, crawls out of the picture.

Méliès' moral philosophy is manichean and his feelings towards the opposite sex are ambivalent. Two kinds of women populated his pantomimes: angels and temptresses. His own favourite rôle was the Devil. As Tzvetan Todorov has pointed out: "the Devil is just another word for libido".[11] Women are everything to Méliès, they are objects of contemplation and externalisations of desire. They can appear from nowhere or change places with flowers, caterpillars, skeletons, coins, bits of paper, ghosts, marble, soap bubbles, their doubles, playing cards, clocks, veils, Jesus Christ, Satan, and, being privileged beings, with Georges Méliès himself.

On the one hand, the Star Film world is an idealised Utopia where women hold a promise and make fabulous appearances as planets, constellations, the moon, astrological symbols, goddesses, sea nymphs, angels, saints, queens and princesses. We are speaking here of 'pure' women, the wholesome and passive kind who inhabit the clouds, grottoes and the sea-bed, who exist among flowers, fruit, shells, animals and insects and who even more intimately exist *as* flora and fauna, as butterflies, birds and fishes. The Arcadian tone of this imagery has its counterpart in the paintings of Henri Rousseau and Louis Eilshemius.

On the other hand, seductive women, the kind that fulfil a promise, appear as ghosts and succubi, the seven deadly sins, as the Devil's agents, and as Satan.

An Arcadian image from
La Fée libellule (1908).

Louis Eilshemius,
Afternoon Wind (1899).
Oil on canvas, 20″ × 36″.

Let us look first at the angels. According to Charles
Fourier, the Utopian socialist, the Butterfly or Alternating
Passion, one of the twelve passions in man, "is the need of
periodic change, contrasting situations, changes of scene,
piquant incidents, novelties apt to create illusions, to stimu-
late both the senses and the soul".[12] Referring, then, to a
certain restlessness or 'flightiness', the butterfly-woman
image also suggests vulnerability, delicacy, fragile beauty,
something to be treated with care. An image from *La Fée
libellule* (1908) captures just this erotic fascination: on the
edge of a lake huge flowers (pansies, lupins, roses, sun-
flowers, honeysuckle) dwarf three butterfly-women. The one
in the foreground, her head tilted slightly, looks straight at
you with dreamy eyes. The butterfly-woman, incidentally,
was part of the iconography of conjuring. Such a creature

That image from *La Fée libellule* (1908).

Marcel Mariën, *Hommage à Méliès* (1968). Collage, 3″ × 3″.

emerged from a chrysalis in Buatier de Kolta's illusion *The Cocoon*, first presented at Maskelyne and Cooke's Egyptian Hall on May 2 1887. It was Buatier de Kolta who inspired Méliès to film his first substitution trick, *The Vanishing Lady* (1896).

Venus emerged from the sea on a shell. In Méliès' films the scallop shell is home not for a bivalve mollusc but for lovely women who display themselves to full advantage. The shell is a sign of femininity, its shape and colouring (the aptly-named Conch of Venus, for example) often mimics the form of the vulva. A woman in a shell is like a pearl in an oyster, and a consistent motif in fairy tales and legends is the one of the virgin from whose mouth pearls and flowers issue. The wind that brings Botticelli's Venus to shore is littered with roses. In Hans Christian Andersen's *The Snow Queen* a princess (that is, a virgin) sits on a pearl as big as a spinning wheel. Mircea Eliade has noted that the act of spinning can represent initiation into the world of adult women: "there is a secret link between feminine initiations, spinning and sexuality."[13]

Telescopes often figure in Star Films and stars take the form of lovely women. Méliès' astronomers (like his alchemists) are bad scientists but sound dreamers. Star-women are out of reach, ethereal, divine. To sit a woman on the moon's crescent is to put her on a pedestal. Like Lucas Cranach, Méliès was aware of the erotic significance of the veil: both wrapped their women in diaphanous fabrics.

Before the black mouths of two caves stands a life-size crucifix on a stone base, together with a skull and a bible. A pitcher of water and a hunk of bread sit on a rock. Straw is strewn on the ground.

Bluette Bernon reclines
on a shell in *The Chimney
Sweep* (1906). Scene 7,
'The Blue Lake. The
Sylphs, the Swimming
Maidens and the Fairies
of the Air.'

Lucas Cranach, *The
Nymph of the Fountain*
(1534).

Veiled women in a
drawing by Méliès from
The Wonderful Living Fan
(1904).

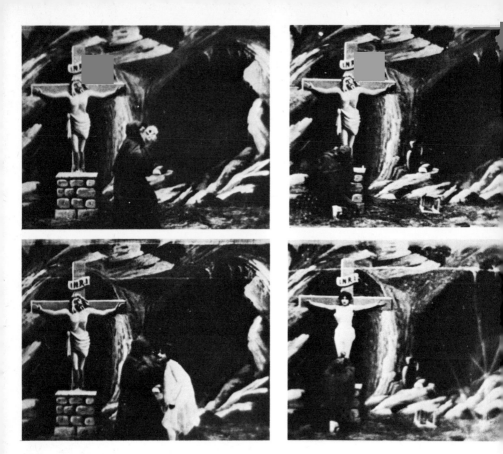

The Temptation of Saint Anthony (1898). A skull changes into the head and body of a maiden (consecutive frame enlargements). And then: one of the most surprising images in cinema (consecutive frame enlargements).

This is the set for *The Temptation of Saint Anthony*. The saint, played by Méliès, dressed in a sackcloth habit, is busy reading the Bible when a woman in a flimsy costume suddenly appears behind him and starts to stroke his beard. He recoils violently, hides his face behind the loose sleeve of his habit and asks for divine aid, which arrives, because the girl promptly vanishes. But when the poor man sits on his stool in an attempt to regain his breath two women (one of them Jehanne d'Alcy) seat themselves on his lap. He jumps up and the demons withdraw. Then the saint rushes over to the skull, a *memento mori*, lifts it to his lips and kisses it twice. At the third embrace the skull becomes a beautiful woman, who is quickly reinforced by two companions. Before disppearing the three graces form a chain and dance around the distraught saint. He makes for the cross but Christ turns into a woman and descends to torment him, at which point an angel arrives. The saint appears to be saved, while Jesus resumes his rightful position on the cross, but the angel is just as desirable as the other phantoms of this ascetic's fevered imagination.

Amidst the disorder of delusion and desire a temptress might be taken for an angel. Méliès was tormented by women just as much as he was fascinated by them—this ambivalence is one reason why he was happy to change them into other objects. Apart from purely Christian soul-searching, Méliès' manichean moral philosophy may have been an intellectualisation of a very real moral dilemma. In her recent gossipy biography, Méliès' granddaughter repeatedly contrasts the qualities of her grandfather's first wife, Eugénie—chaste, retiring and homely—with his mistress, later his second wife, Fanny—worldly, demanding and ardent. Méliès was to gravitate between the two until Eugénie's death in 1913.

Méliès liked playing the Devil most of all. His pantomime demon personifies the subversive spirit of eroticism, whose appearance causes havoc and whose enemies are quick to subdue him. In *Beelzebub's Daughters, or The Women of Fire*, made in 1903, a good year for demons, a Devil forms three "mystic maidens" by moulding the flames that issue from his hands. Lovely women are often created and live like salamanders amidst fire and smoke. The liveliness, the heat, and the destructive potential of fire make it an erotic symbol for ardent, sensual womanhood. The chaste woman, on the other hand, is destroyed by fire, as is Joan of Arc, whose life Méliès filmed in 1900, and the female victim in *A Miracle*

Maskelyne's Mephisto, in a detail from an Egyptian Hall poster for the illusion *Arcana* (1887).

Méliès as Mephistopheles.

Under the Inquisition (1904), of whom nothing remains but ashes. Méliès' Devil is also the cinema's first mad scientist, although a genial savant who has the ability to create life, usually in the shape of beautiful women. In *The Devil in A Convent* (1899), Satan takes on an erotic vampire rôle and assumes the form of a bat: "The Devil jumps forth from the Holy Water font, amid a column of smoke issuing from same, and flies gently to the ground by spreading his cloak as the wings of a bat."[14]

Like Freud's primal father who kept all the females for himself, Méliès often chose to be the only man in his films, while surrounding himself with women. Perhaps a certain patriarchal egotism, complemented by an employer's low opinion of the abilities of his workers, may explain everything.*

Stag films found an early place in the cinema, and strip-tease was a popular subject. Charles Pathé's 'broad scenes of a piquant nature' formed one of the twelve genres in his catalogue. Of course the heroines of such Pathé films as *The Undressing of the Model* (1897) and *The Flea* wore maillots (flesh-coloured body stockings). In many of the popular arts of the day tableaux based upon famous contemporary paintings were used as a pretext for presenting the nearly-naked female form. In the theatre

> numerous authors—whose reputations were not always bad—composed sketches and pantomimes that had but one purpose: to introduce the nude . . . At the Folies-Bergère, the Moulin Rouge, the Olympia, the Variétés and Bobinos, tableaux vivants inspired by the masterpieces of academic art, were preferred. Thomas Couture's *La Décadence romaine* and Ingres' *Le Bain turc* were reconstituted at great cost.[15]

In the cinema, Pathé's *The Awakening of Chrysis* (1899), for instance, was based upon Manet's *Olympia*. It was in this form that paintings exhibited in the Salons made the trip to the fairground cinemas. Cinematography had begun to play its part in the dissemination of kitsch.

Méliès was no exception. Here is a synopsis of *While Under the Hypnotist's Influence* (1897):

Scene—in the consultation room of a hypnotist, showing

* "In the trick routines, however, he always took the leading rôle, for he could never make his players understand the thousand and one skills needed for a complicated trick to work well." (Georges Méliès, *Mes Mémoires*).

the approach of a subject, who, while under his mysterious influence, is subjected to all manner of tests. She falls prone on to the floor, but is picked up while in this position and placed across two chairs, her head resting on one, her heels on the other. While in this position her clothes mysteriously remove themselves to several hooks on the wall, until she is finally left in an almost nude condition. The chair is suddenly jerked from under her feet and head, and she falls flat upon the floor with great force. She is brought to, and while protesting against her unclad condition, the hypnotist takes the clothes from the hook upon which they are suspended and throws them on his subject, who immediately appears as fully dressed as when she entered the apartment.[16]

A Peeping Tom at the Seaside, A Private Dinner, After the Ball, and *An Irritable Model* were all made in 1897. *The Bridegroom's Dilemma* (1899), with Méliès and Mlle Bairal, was, according to an understatement in the Warwick Film Catalogue, "an excellent film, full of surprises and illusions, the exhibition of which will certainly be welcomed at any Smoking Concert or Stag Party. Space forbids a detailed description." Méliès was well aware of the sex-appeal of his danseuses, chorus girls who appear barely disguised as soldiers or sailors. In *The Chimney Sweep* (1906), for example, 'The Ping-Pongs', an English troupe, appeared as the Troops of Dream Country. Occasionally the sauciness of a Star Film was less overt, as when the eclipsing of two planets, one male, the other female, in *The Eclipse* (1907), caused the female one—"dainty Diana"—to smile contentedly.

After the Ball (1897). Jehanne d'Alcy at left and Jeanne Brady.

The eroticism in Méliès' films is to be found in his earlier theatrical productions as well. Women take the form of planets and goddesses in *The Moon's Pranks*, evolve from flowers in *The Fairy of the Flowers* and appear in the form of "living and impalpable spectres" in *The Mysterious Page* and *Spirit Phenomena*.

The Journey

The Star Film Catalogue sets the scene for *An Adventurous Automobile Trip* (1905, eleven minutes) thus:

> King Leopold of Belgium has come to Paris to renew his acquaintances among the dainty 'Parisiennes' who for some time past have known how to appreciate his great fondness for their society. He ardently desires to make a trip to Monte Carlo, the celebrated watering place and gambling resort in the principality of Monaco, but his time is so limited that he cannot give up the seventeen hours necessary for the trip by express from Paris to the Riviera. He chances to meet, wholly by accident, an automobile manufacturer who makes a proposition to accomplish the journey in three hours, and it is this sursurprisingly rapid journey which is portrayed by the cinematograph.

The first scene is dominated by the painted image of a garage, the end one of a line of shops, the façade of which bears the advertisements and the Star Film copyright sign. A couple of mechanics pass the time of day with some passing women. From the right an automobile enters and pulls up. In it sit the king and his driver, sporting long beards and long fur coats. A huge metal funnel is brought forward and a chain of mechanics pass can after can of petrol to the king who pours it into the funnel. His aide, prostrate while checking the underneath of the vehicle, receives a face full of petrol when the king's attention is distracted by a gentleman prodding him with an umbrella. The mechanics howl with laughter at this. Soon a crowd of about fifteen people gathers, filling the stage. The king is about to depart, but when he lets off the handbrake the car runs backwards, completely flattening a gendarme. The king departs, leaving the townspeople to resurrect the unfortunate man with car pumps. The suit of clothes representing the flattened policeman 'breathes' with each influx of air. The crowd gradually surround the figure, obscuring it. When they draw back we see the gendarme on the brink of resurrection. The people gather round again. Suddenly there is a tremendous explosion that knocks most of them to the ground. Cut to scene 2: the Place de l'Opéra, the opera house in the background, painted on the backcloth. A number of gendarmes are holding back a crowd of about twenty bourgeois men and women. The king's car enters, to the delight of the crowd. A number of people come forward in turn to greet the monarch: they are, in reality, M. Notté, a singer at the Opéra, Galipaux, the actor, 'The Giant Swede' (at least seven-and-a-half feet tall) and Victor de Cottens. One of them is 'Little Tich', a midget wearing a loud check jacket, top hat and 3-feet long shoes in which he shuffles across the stage towards the giant. To get a light from the giant's cigarette 'Little Tich' stands on the tip of his yard-long shoes. To the frenzied goodbyes of the merry crowd the car exits left.

Cut to scene 3: a roadside scene painted on a backdrop—hills, a house with steps leading up to it, a milestone, signpost, bench, a hut against which a shovel leans. The foreground is occupied by a cutout painted as rocks. In the distance we see the tiny car (a model) skirt the brow of a hill right to left. Then a larger car (another model) crosses the middle distance left to right. A village postman (Méliès) with a beard, straw hat and box of letters, enters, followed by the automobile, which runs him down. He is tossed (at least a dummy is) right over the top of the vehicle. He picks himself up and shakes a fist at the departed car. We leave him picking up his letters.

Dissolve to scene 4: painted peaks occupy the whole screen, no stage is visible. The car (a model) crosses the mountain range in a lengthy tracking shot. The car leaps a chasm and tumbles over a precipice.

Dissolve to scene 5: a toll-gate in the city-wall of Dijon. Two officers stand before sentry boxes. Their job is to search the belongings of any traveller entering the city, for levies have to be paid on any combustibles carried. A couple of tradesmen are

An Adventurous Automobile Trip (1905). Above left: 'Little Tich' in his big boots measures up to 'The Giant Swede' (frame enlargement). Above right: model work in scene 3 (frame enlargement).

searched. A superior officer, a fat man with an enormous protruding belly, comes on the scene, knocking over one of his subordinates. The automobile appears and runs up against the chief's paunch which prevents it entering the gates. Indeed, the car bounces off the man. Reinforcements soon arrive, but six officers are not enough—when the car hits the fat official, he explodes, and it departs leaving a cloud of smoke and a number of prostrate gendarmes in its wake.

Dissolve to scene 6: on the backcloth a seascape with yachts and rocks is painted. An arch of rock and a wall stand behind two stalls, where ladies in local costume are selling fruit and ribbon to a couple of passers-by, who flee when they 'see' a speeding auto off-screen. A figure carrying a pile of boxes comes diving on stage, followed by the car, which demolishes the stalls. A crowd of people appear and begin to pick up the scattered fruit. For no apparent reason a free-for-all develops, and in the last instance the target for all missiles is the old fruit-seller.

Dissolve to scene 7: a village street, bounded by a rear wall with a rickety gate, on one side a wall with a large gate and a dangerous corner, on the other side a house. A courting couple enter, cross the stage, peer round the corner of the house, then turn and run, pursued by a panicking crowd. Naturally, the auto appears and drives straight through the large gate, demolishing the wall in the process. The crowd regroups to deplore such bad driving.

Cut to scene 8: a woodcutter's yard. The backcloth is painted to represent a hut flanked by trees and an enormous heap of cut timber. All is activity: a woodcutter cuts timber, a gardener, in straw hat and long apron, fills his watering can, outdoor diners boisterously charge their glasses. Suddenly over the roof of the greenhouse the car appears, flies through the air (a mechanical feat this) and lands on the luncheon table, demolishing everything in sight.

Cut to scene 9: the whole of this scene is shot out of doors, a lawn with shrubbery forming the 'stage'. A painted backcloth represents a seascape, with rocks and palm-trees. Two peasants, the sun shining noticeably on their straw hats, take their leave of a third. The scene remains empty for several moments before a team of white horses appear on the right, drawing a wagon. (At this moment a woman steps accidentally into camera. Startled, she turns and retreats briskly.) The wagon bears a tank labelled 'Coal Tar—Sté Anonyme du Goudron—Theer Gesellschaft'. Suddenly the inevitable automobile enters and demolishes the wagon in a cloud of smoke, the tar-seller turning a spectacular somersault in the process.

Cut to scene 10: again shot outside, on the same stretch of lawn. On the left is a rostrum decorated with ribbons and flowers. To the right is a kiosk, or bandstand. The backcloth is a view of Monte Carlo. Two dancers in local costume perform before the welcoming committee of fifteen, seated in the rostrum. They are shooed away by energetic gendarmes. The arrival of the king's car is announced by a frenzied character in a tweed suit. When it appears the auto mounts the stairs of the tribune and does a backward bound through the air out of frame. Appearing once more the car draws up to the rostrum steps, colliding with them and knocking over part of the edifice. Notwithstanding the destruction it has caused, the automobile and its occupants are fêted by a madly waving crowd, including several policemen.

The car about to crash into the tar wagon and the flying automobile about to demolish the rostrum. *An Adventurous Automobile Trip* (frame enlargements).

Méliès' travelogues are his most majestic productions, on a spectacular scale, sometimes consisting of thirty or more scenes, and lasting 15–20 minutes. The simple linear structure of the journey 'from A to B' lent itself to the simple linear construction of Star Films: there is a sort of 'pantographic' relationship between the metres of film expended and the kilometres of road or ocean or space to be covered.

Méliès was among the first to explore the imagery of *arrival and departure*, in a series of 1896 films photographed à la Lumière: *Arrival of a Train in Vincennes Station*, *Boat Leaving the Harbour at Trouville* and *Automobile Starting on a Race*. Like a number of contemporary painters (Monet, Pissarro, Seurat and Marquet), the early film-makers turned to the city streets, harbours, railway termini and rivers for their imagery. It was there that things *moved*.

Chivalrous quests come from the fairy story. Méliès' picaresque tales, searches for fame and fortune and sentimental love, have basically the same construction: before marrying a youth must undergo a trial involving unknown dangers; before departing on it he is given a talisman; the journey is full of marvels and monsters; and marriage follows the successful resolution of his quest. We could read this narrative as a fable about a young man's sexual initiation, but it is the imagery of the quest itself that is more compelling. Much of *Fairyland, or the Kingdom of the Fairies* (1903), for example, takes place on the seabed. It was shot through an aquarium with real fish swimming in it, a device Méliès used more than once. Prince Bel Azor is attempting to rescue his betrothed, Princess Azurine, who has been abducted by a witch and locked in a tower in the middle of the ocean. Their galley wrecked, the prince and his retainers find themselves on the floor of the sea. They are led to Neptune's Court by the Fairy of the Waters who supplies them with marvellous transportation: Bel Azor sits astride a sturgeon, his major-domo on a lobster, while his servants ride on chariots drawn by fish. They pass through a series of tableaux that fade one into the other, from the Palace of Lobsters through the Azure Grotto to Neptune's Court, where they witness a pageant of naiads, genii and tritons, recumbent in scallop shells. The last stage of the party's journey takes place in the belly of a friendly whale which regurgitates them on to dry land.

In *The Palace of the Arabian Nights* (1905) Prince Charming, searching for the treasure he must possess before he can marry Aouda, the Rajah's daughter, is helped by Khalafar, a genie he released from an urn. They travel down the Sacred River in the company of the Blue Dwarf, then the High Priest cuts a path through the dense foliage of the Magic Forest. The Fairy of Gold leads the Prince through the Wonderful Caverns to the Crystal Grotto where unfriendly spirits set upon them. In the Miraculous Caves—an "exact reproduction of the celebrated 'Elephantine Cave' in British India"[17]—the Prince, armed with a magic sword, beats off a dragon and a host of enormous toads which turn into stone. The Prince has come through the test: "Horrible visions are going to terminate and give way to some charming apparitions."[18] The stone monsters change into lotuses, from which emerge the Goddesses of the Lower World. A series of dissolves leads us through a rotunda with its fountain of fire, the Temple of Gold, into the Palace of the Arabian Nights, where Prince Charming secures the vital treasure, which is paraded upon litters carried by "a sumptuous cortège of Bayardères, vestals, princesses and others".[19]

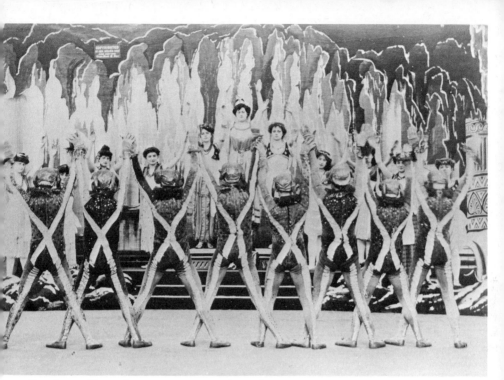

In these disarming pageants, Méliès the thaumaturge wanted to evoke a sense of wonder and admiration in his audiences, which comprised the working and lower-middle classes of all ages and nationalities. To do this he linked a series of spectacular tableaux. The chivalrous quest proved a readily recognised and conveniently assimilated genre for doing this.

The Palace of the Arabian Nights (1905). Scene 23, 'The Goddesses of the Lower Regions'.

The sceptical tone of Méliès' *ludicrous expeditions* is in complete contrast to the Utopian serenity of his chivalrous quests. It is Jules Verne, rather than Charles Fourier, that they invoke: "Jules Verne Outdone"[20] was the claim made for *An Impossible Voyage* (1904). Between 1863 and his death in 1905 Verne wrote more than one hundred novels in an attempt to summarise all the geographical, geological, physical and astronomical knowledge amassed by contemporary science. In a biography of her uncle, Marguérite Allotte de la Fuÿe wrote:

If one had to classify his hundred and four books . . according to their nature and content, it would not be unfair to group them under these four headings: novels terrestial, aerial, aquatic and igneous; terms which correspond besides, with the four components he had detected in himself in his youthful fervour: wisdom, observation, depth, ethical insight.[21]

'Films terrestrial, aerial, aquatic and igneous' could apply to Méliès' travelogues too, but their similarity to Verne's is superficial. Méliès was closer to the Carroll of *The Hunting of the Snark*, the Jarry of *The Exploits and Opinions of Doctor Faustroll* and the Roussel of *Impressions of Africa*. His films are parodies of Verne's sober romances, and of the world they describe. Verne's *voyages extraordinaires* became Méliès' *ludicrous expeditions*.

In the illustrations accompanying *20,000 Leagues Under the Sea* the hero, Arronax, is represented in the likeness of the young, beardless Verne. Georges Méliès elected himself leader, hero and brains behind the trips undertaken by his intrepid scientists to the surface of the moon and sun. *A Trip to the Moon* and *An Impossible Voyage* are identical in structure: after the plans are revealed at a savant's club and a visit paid to a foundry, the explorers set off for outer space; they reach their goal, survive thanks to the resourcefulness of their leader, but are obliged to return to earth; they land in the sea, are rescued, and fêted.

An obsessive image from these films (and in *An Adventurous Automobile Trip*) is the collision. The image of the crash demonstrates that the magician destroys things in order to prove his own harmlessness. Méliès' imaginary races (automobile and otherwise) found their counterpart in reality in madcap journeys that emphasised the element of play typical of an emergent technology. Huizinga speaks of the "sporting side of almost every triumph of commerce and technology: the highest turnover, the greatest tonnage, the fastest crossing, the greatest altitude, etc. Here a purely ludic element has, for once, got the better of utilitarian considerations."[22] Jules Verne built adventure stories around these playful races (*Around the World in 80 Days*); Jean du Taillis reported them as they happened (*Pékin–Paris automobile en 80 jours*); Alfred Jarry burlesqued them (*The Supermale, The Passion Considered As An Uphill Bicycle Race*). Méliès' sympathies lay, so to speak, with Jarry.

A Terrible Night is one of Méliès' earliest films, made in 1896. It is shot in the open air, in bright sunlight. Hanging curtains form a backcloth. A bed, occupying most of the scene, is flanked by a wicker chair and cupboard with a candle on it to the left, and a wooden chair with folded clothes on it to the right. A rug is spread before the bed.

The crash. *An Impossible Voyage* (1904). Scene 22, 'Terrible Telescoping'.

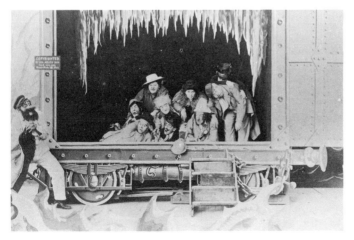

Crazyloff/Méliès, the resourceful leader from the Institute of Incoherent Geography. *An Impossible Voyage* (1904). Scene 29, 'The Thaw'.

A traveller in a black beard and white nightgown and cap arranges his clothes on the chair and climbs into bed. He blows out the candle although it gets no darker (the sun continues to shine). A huge beetle, about 9-inches long, begins to climb up the sheets. When the bug leaps on to the rear curtains the traveller grabs a broom, swipes at it, knocks it on his bed, whereupon he leaps up and treads on it, placing the insect's body in the bedside cupboard. He gets out of bed, picks up his shoe and kills several more beetles.

Dreamed travels form a further classification of the journey in Méliès' films. Anxiety and wish fulfilment, common to dreams, are qualities to be found in most Star Films. The dreams dreamed by the dormant protagonists of *The Chimney Sweep* (1906) and *Grandmother's Story* (1908) are undisguised wish fulfilments. In the former, Jack the chimney-sweep dreams of a journey through Utopia and of being crowned king. In the latter, a little girl dreams of an expedition to Toyland and the realm of King Sweet. Other sleeping heroes can experience anxiety dreams. In *Under the Seas* (1907)

The cross-sectional set in *Tunneling the English Channel* (1907). Scene 4, 'Good Night'.

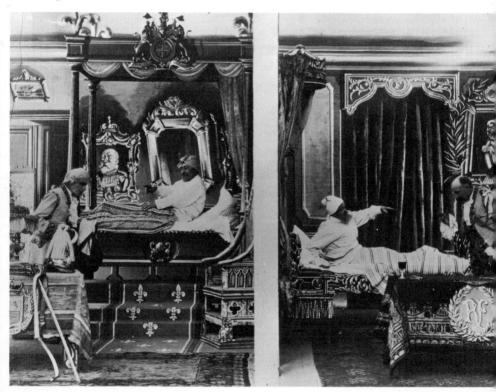

Yves the fisherman's journey along the seabed takes an alarming turn when he is chased by monstrous fish. On awakening he needs a stiff drink. In *Tunnelling the English Channel* (1907), King Edward VII and President Fallières of France dream simultaneously of building a Channel Tunnel. All goes well with the project until a catastrophic accident awakens both dreamers. As a result of their premonitions the two men decide to postpone the project. Incidentally, this film is interesting for Méliès' formal innovation of the cross-sectional set. Instead of using consecutive shots to show the king and president in their respective bed-chambers Méliès presents us with one set divided by a central wall, on each side of which one man performs in unison with the other. The comical effect of this presages in a curious way the mirror sequence between the Marx Brothers in *Duck Soup*.

From time to time a *journey to perdition* serves as the apotheosis of a melodrama or comedy. Such is the case in *The Wandering Jew* (1904). Isaac Laquedem, condemned to walk forever for having refused water to Christ *en route* to Calvary, is assailed by guilty memories, Satan, an angel and terrible

The Wandering Jew (1904). Scene 3, 'The Cliffs of Despond' with Méliès at left.

weather, "but on he plods . . . he plods . . . he plods throughout the succession of the centuries".[23] It is amusing to observe that, like Méliès, the unfortunate Jew was once a shoemaker! *The Merry Frolics of Satan* (1906) is a variation of the Faust legend. After an eventful trip through outer space the engineer Crackford, whose time on this earth has run out, is roasted on Satan's turnspit.

Chases were a speciality of the early English cinema.

Earnest films of pursuit, capture and rescue were made by men like James Williamson, Frank Mottershaw and Cecil Hepworth. Méliès made the occasional comic chase film. When he did so, he made a noise about it: *The Chimney Sweep* had, according to the Star Film Catalogue, "Comedy—Mystery—Sensational Adventures—Pathos—Acrobatics—Spectacular Effects and A GREAT BIG CHASE". In *Robert Macaire and Bertrand* (1906) two thieves are pursued by the police through earthquake and outer space, on foot, train and balloon, before making their escape.

Robert Macaire and Bertrand (1906). Scene 9, 'A Terrible Earthquake'.

One of the recurrent images of the journey is of the *bewildered traveller*. A fatigued visitor to *The Bewitched Inn* (1897) finds that his garments assume a life of their own after he has taken them off, and the guests *At the Hotel Mix-Up* (1908) see their clothes heaped in a pile and burned by a zealous valet. A meal interrupted by demolition of the dining-room is a further embellishment of the frustrated diner image we noted earlier. A passing car or balloon usually accomplishes this.

"A true poet wants imagination to be a voyage," said Gaston Bachelard: "Thus each poet owes us his invitation to the voyage . . . The sequence of images arranged by the invitation to the voyage takes on, through the aptness of its order, a special vivacity that makes it possible to designate . . . a movement of the imagination. This movement is not just a metaphor. We can actually feel it within ourselves, usually as a lightening, an effortless imagination of connected images, an eagerness to pursue the enchanting dream."[24]

The demolition of a dinner table in *An Adventurous Automobile Trip* (1905). Scene 8, 'Over the Conservatory'.

Méliès' violent and funny films exist in the exhilarating area where opposites find their resolution, destruction giving way to restitution, malevolence to benevolence, and fragmentation to continuity. The whole dynamic process is perceived in a state induced by the monotonous, relentless objectivity of his formal style: a state of reverie, ideal for the reception and appreciation of Méliès' genial poetry.

The Writing on the Wall

"When I've smoked a cigarette I'm not in the habit of retaining the butt."—Francis Picabia

Georges Méliès has long suffered the indignity of being considered the cinema's venerable grandpa, kindly, amusing, but largely irrelevant. The young men of today have preferred to come to grips with the 'fathers' of the medium. The reactionary philosophy (masquerading as 'humanism') and the stern and sober pomposity of directors like John Ford* makes them natural candidates for all that oedipal curiosity. Meanwhile, Méliès is known as the mechanic who invented all those clever tricks but who wasn't bright enough to move the camera about, or as the clown whose theatrical narratives, though picturesque, are childish and largely insignificant. His greatest claim to their attention has been that he influenced Edwin S. Porter.

Rather, we have shown that Méliès' 'weaknesses' are his great strengths; that his relentless style, unbroken by montage but enlivened by spectacular camera tricks, is admirably effective in inducing a condition of absent- and open-mindedness propitious for the reception of his poetic imagery; that this imagery, *because* it is childish, is bursting with vitality, operating in that dynamic area of tension and release, of dislocation and relocation that we call the marvellous.

The inclination that Méliès felt to make detail the focus of his work is not a limitation. Instead it suggests a way of looking at cinema as a medium only as valuable as its occasional revelatory image. The wider framework of narrative structure we discard without reservation or guilt, in favour of the metamorphic, the erotic and the humorous image.

Gérard Lenne has said that the true function of the fantasy film is to pulverise the semantic prison "which is nothing less than the reflection and symptom of many others".[1] The

---

* "In the history of American films, no name shines more brightly than that of John Ford. He represents the best in American films and the best in America." (Richard Nixon).

superficial indifference that Méliès holds for the identity of things, and for their names, reveals a deeper concern in his willingness to grant objects complete semantic liberty in ceaselessly transforming them into other objects. And this semantic liberty might, to paraphrase Lenne, be a way to other freedoms. Far from being obsolete, Georges Méliès' vision is full of promise.

Phantoms . . . R.I.P.
Drawing by Georges
Méliès.

Appendix I
REFERENCES

DARKENED ROOMS

1   Georges Méliès, *Les Vues cinématographiques,* 1907; quoted in Georges Sadoul, *Georges Méliès,* Éditions Seghers, Paris, 1962, p. 115.

2   Stan Brakhage, *Art Forum,* New York, January 1973, p. 76.

3   Gaston Bachelard, *Poetics of Space,* Beacon Press, Boston, 1964, p. 47.

4   André Breton, preface to Pierre Mabille, *Le Miroir du merveilleux,* Éditions de Minuit, Paris, 1962, p. 16.

5   Gérard Lenne, *Le Cinéma fantastique et ses mythologies,* Éditions du Cerf, Paris, 1970, p. 15.

6   Maurice Bessy and G. M. Lo Duca, *Georges Méliès, mage,* Prisma, Paris, 1945; 2nd edition J. J. Pauvert, Paris, 1961; page references apply to the 2nd edition.

7   Maurice Bessy, *Méliès,* Anthologie du Cinéma 11, Paris, 1966.

8   Georges Sadoul, op. cit.

9   Jacques Deslandes, *Le Boulevard du Cinéma à l'époque de Georges Méliès,* Éditions du Cerf, Paris, 1963.

10   Jacques Deslandes and Jacques Richard, *Histoire comparée du cinéma,* tome II, Casterman, Paris, 1968.

11   Madeleine Malthête-Méliès, *Georges Méliès, créateur du spectacle cinématographie,* privately printed, Paris, 1961; 2nd edition, Paris, 1966.

12   Madeleine Malthête-Méliès, *Méliès l'enchanteur,* Hachette, Paris, 1973.

LIFE AND WORK (1861–1938)

1   Maurice Donnay, *Le Lycée Louis-le-Grand,* Gallimard, Paris, 1939, p. 96.

2   Georges Méliès, *Mes Mémoires,* Rome, 1938; reprinted in the original French in Maurice Bessy and G. M. Lo Duca, op. cit., p. 173. Written in the third person.

3   Ibid.

4   Madeleine Malthête-Méliès, *Méliès l'enchanteur,* pp. 49–56.

5   Nevil Maskelyne and David Devant, *Our Magic,* Routledge, London, 1912, pp. 95 and 96.

6   Georges Méliès, *Passez Muscade,* no. 43, Lyons, 1928, pp. 515–16.

7   Georges Méliès, *L'Orchestre,* Paris, March 10 1890; quoted in Jacques Deslandes, op. cit., p. 37.

8   Georges Méliès, *L'Orchestre,* Paris, March 9 1891; quoted in Jacques Deslandes, op. cit., p. 40.

9   Georges Méliès, *L'Orchestre,* Paris, October 2 1892; quoted in Jacques Deslandes, op. cit., p. 43.

10   Georges Méliès, *L'Orchestre,* Paris, June 10 1892; quoted in Jacques Deslandes, op. cit., pp. 42–3.

11 Georges Méliès, *Mes Mémoires*, p. 175.

12 Ibid., p. 173.

13 Georges Sadoul, op. cit., p. 166.

14 Georges Méliès, *Mes Mémoires*, p. 187.

15 *Warwick Film Catalogue*, London, 1901, pp. 57–8.

16 Georges Méliès, *Mes Mémoires*, pp. 185–6.

17 *Warwick Film Catalogue*, p. 58.

18 Anatole Jakovski, *Éros du dimanche*, J. J. Pauvert, Paris, 1964, p. 237.

19 Maurice Bessy and G. M. Lo Duca, op. cit., p. 144.

20 David Devant, *My Magic Life*, Hutchinson, London, 1931, pp. 167–8.

21 E. G. Robertson, *Mémoires récréatifs, scientifiques et anecdotiques*, Chez l'auteur et la Librairie de Wartz, Paris, 1831 (vol. I), 1833 (vol. II), vol. I, pp. 294–304.

22 G. M. Lo Duca, *Le Dessin animé*, Prisma, Paris, p. 128.

23 *Warwick Film Catalogue*, p. 72.

24 *Star Film Catalogue*, New York, 1903–8; incoherent pagination.

25 Ibid.

26 *Charles Urban Trading Company Catalogue*, London, 1903, p. 142.

27 *Star Film Catalogue*.

28 Georges Méliès, *L'Importance du scénario*, 1932; quoted in Georges Sadoul, op. cit., pp. 115–16.

29 Walter Benjamin, *The Work of Art in the Age of Mechanical Reproduction*, in *Illuminations*, Schocken Books, New York, 1968, p. 225.

30 Georges Méliès, *En marge de l'histoire du cinématographe*, 1920; quoted in Jacques Deslandes and Jacques Richard, op. cit., p. 426.

31 *Charles Urban Trading Company Catalogue*, London, 1905, p. 303.

32 *Star Film Catalogue*.

33 Victor de Cottens, *Paris, dont je rêvais*, Garnier-Flachat, Vichy, 1948.

34 Jacques Deslandes, op. cit., p. 48.

35 *Star Film Catalogue*.

36 Ibid.

37 *The Moving Picture World*, New York, October 17 1908, p. 304.

38 Georges Méliès, quoted in Georges Sadoul, op. cit., pp. 70–1.

39 *The Moving Picture World*, October 23 1909, p. 561.

40 *The Moving Picture World*, March 26 1910.

41 Bernard Rosenberg and Harry Silverstein, *The Real Tinsel*, Macmillan, New York, 1970, p. 324.

42 Charles Pathé, *De Pathé Frères à Pathé Cinéma*, Premier Plan, Lyons, 1970, pp. 43–5.

43 Francis Lacassin, *Out of Oblivion. Alice Guy Blaché*, *Sight and Sound*, London, summer 1971, p. 152.

44 Georges Méliès, *Mes Mémoires*, p. 177.

45 Georges Méliès, *La Sêmeuse*, privately printed, 1916.

46 Georges Méliès, *Mes Mémoires*, p. 205.

47 Georges Méliès, quoted in Georges Sadoul, op. cit., p. 143.

1 Lewis Carroll, *Sylvie and Bruno*, in *The Complete Works of Lewis Carroll*, The Nonesuch Press, London, 1966, p. 436.

2 André R. Maugé, quoted in Georges Méliès, *Mes Mémoires*, p. 217.

3 Georges Méliès, quoted in Georges Sadoul, op. cit., p. 144.

4 Nevil Maskelyne and David Devant, op. cit., pp. 226 ff.

5 Jacques Deslandes and Jacques Richard, op. cit., p. 187.

6 Madeleine Malthête-Méliès, *Film Culture*, no. 48/49, New York, 1970.

7 Ado Kyrou, *Le Surréalisme au cinéma*, 2nd edition, Le Terrain Vague, Paris, 1963.

8 Charlie Chaplin, quoted on the dust-jacket of Maurice Bessy and G. M. Lo Duca, op. cit.

9 *Star Film Catalogue.*

10 Milbourne Christopher, *Panorama of Magic*, Dover Books, New York, 1962, p. 1.

11 Tzvetan Todorov, *Introduction à la littérature fantastique*, Éditions du Seuil, Paris, 1970, p. 134.

12 Charles Fourier, *Théorie de l'unité universelle*, Paris, 1841–3; quoted in Jonathan Beecher and Richard Bienvenue, *The Utopian Vision of Charles Fourier*, Beacon Press, Boston, 1971, p. 219.

13 Mircea Eliade, *Myths, Dreams and Mysteries*, Fontana Library, London, 1968, p. 215.

14 *Warwick Film Catalogue*, p. 63.

15 Patrick Waldberg, *Éros Modern Style*, J. J. Pauvert, Paris, 1964, pp. 111 and 113.

16 *Warwick Film Catalogue*, p. 58.

17 *Star Film Catalogue.*

18 Ibid.

19 Ibid.

20 Ibid.

21 Marguerite Allotte de la Fuÿe, *Jules Verne: His Life and Work*, Staples Press, London, 1954, ch. XIII.

22 Johan Huizinga, *Homo Ludens*, Paladin, London, 1970, p. 226.

23 *Star Film Catalogue.*

24 Gaston Bachelard, *L'Air et les songes*, Paris, 1962; quoted in *On Poetic Imagination and Reverie. Selections From the Work of Gaston Bachelard*, Bobbs-Merrill, Indianapolis–New York, 1971, pp. 21–2.

THE WRITING ON THE WALL

1 Gérard Lenne, op. cit., p. 17.

Appendix II

GEORGES MÉLIÈS TRICKOGRAPHY

This trickography is based on the one in Jacques Deslandes, *Le Boulevard du Cinéma à l'époque de Georges Méliès*, pp. 34–49. The English titles are my own.

1888
La Stroubaïka Persane/The Persian Stroubaïka (October)

1889
La Page Mystérieuse/The Mysterious Page (October)
La Fée des Fleurs ou le Miroir de Cagliostro/The Fairy of the Flowers or Cagliostro's Mirror (October)
L'Enchanteur Alcofrisbas/Alcofrisbas the Enchanter (December)

1890
Le Valet de Trèfle vivant/The Living Jack of Clubs (January)
Hypnotisme, Catalepsie, Magnétisme/Hypnotism, Catalepsy, Magnetism (March)
Le Manoir du Diable/The Devil's Castle (September)
Le Nain jaune/The Yellow Dwarf (December)

1891
American Spiritualistic Mediums ou le Décapité récalcitrant/American Spiritualistic Mediums or the Recalcitrant Decapitated Man (March)
Les Farces de la Lune ou les Mésaventures de Nostradamus/The Moon's Pranks, or the Misadventures of Nostradamus (July)
Le Calife de Bagdad/The Caliph of Baghdad (December)

1892
Le Charlatan fin de siècle/An Up-to-Date Mountebank (June)
La Source enchantée/The Enchanted Spring (October)
Le daï Kang (December)

1893
Isis (December)
La Caverne des Gnomes/The Gnomes' Cavern (December)
L'Escarpolette Polonaise/The Polish Swing (December)

1894
L'Auberge du Diable/The Devil's Inn (May)
Le Château de Mesmer/Mesmer's Castle (December)

1895
Le Rêve de Coppelius/Coppelius' Dream (October)
Thomas Oldboot (December)

1896
Le Pilori/The Pillory (January)
Le Miracle du Brahmine/The Brahmin's Miracle (February)
Les Rayons Roentgen/A Novice at X-Rays (March)
Le Mystère de Memphis ou la Résurrection de Cléopâtre/Mystery at Memphis or Cleopatra's Resurrection (December)

1897
La Cage d'or/The Golden Cage (January)

1905
Le nouveau miracle du Brahmine/The Brahmin's New Miracle

1907
Osiris
Le Diable vert/The Green Devil
Les Phenomènes du Spiritisme/Spirit Phenomena

The above is printed by kind permission of Jacques Deslandes and his publishers, Les Editions du Cerf.

Appendix III

GEORGES MÉLIÈS FILMOGRAPHY

This filmography was prepared by consulting the following sources:

Star Film Catalogue, 1903–8.
Warwick Film Catalogue, 1901.
Charles Urban Trading Company Catalogue, 1903, 1904, 1905.
The Moving Picture World, 1908–10.
Maurice Bessy and G. M. Lo Duca, *Georges Méliès, mage*.
Georges Sadoul, *An Index to the Creative Work of Georges Méliès*, special supplement to *Sight and Sound*, London, 1947.
Georges Sadoul, *Georges Méliès*.
Howard Lamarr Walls, *Motion Pictures 1894–1912*, Library of Congress, Washington, 1953.
Jacques Deslandes, *Le Boulevard du Cinéma à l'époque de Georges Méliès*.
P. Tainguy (for Georges Méliès), letters to Léon Gaumont, Jacques Deslandes Collection.

The film's French title is preceded by its *Star Film Catalogue* number and followed by the American and English titles respectively. If the month of release is known, it is mentioned next. Finally the length in metres and feet is given. Titles marked with an asterisk are those of extant films.

1896

1 Une Partie de cartes/Playing Cards (May) [20 metres/65 feet]
2 Séance de prestidigitation/Conjuring [20/65]
3 Plus fort que le maître/Smarter Than the Teacher [20/65]
4 Jardinier brûlant des herbes/Gardener Burning Weeds [20/65]
5 Les Chevaux de bois/A Merry-go-Round [20/65]
6 L'Arroseur/Watering the Flowers [20/65]
7 Les Blanchisseuses/The Washerwomen [20/65]
8 Arrivée d'un train Gare de Vincennes/Arrival of a Train at Vincennes Station [20/65]
9 Le Chiffonier/Une bonne farce/The Rag-Picker/A Good Joke [20/65]
10 Place de l'Opéra. 1er aspect/Place de l'Opéra, 1st View [20/65]
11 Place du Théâtre Français/ditto [20/65]
12 Un Petit Diable/A Little Devil [20/65]
13 Couronnement de la Rosière/Coronation of a Village Maiden [20/65]
14 Bébé et fillettes/Baby and Young Girls [20/65]
15 Défense d'afficher/Post No Bills [20/65]
16 Bateau-Mouche sur la Seine/Steamboats on River Seine [20/65]
17 Place de l'Opéra. 2e aspect/Place de l'Opéra, 2nd View [20/65]
18 Boulevard des Italiens/ditto [20/65]
19 Un Lycée de jeunes filles/Academy for Young Ladies [20/65]
20 Bois de Boulogne (Touring Club)/ditto [20/65]
21 Bois de Boulogne (Porte de Madrid)/ditto [20/65]
22 Sauvetage en rivière/Rescue on the River (1st part) [20/65]
23 Sauvetage en rivière/Rescue on the River (2nd part) [20/65]

24 Le Régiment/French Regiment Going to the Parade [20/65]
25 Campement de bohémiens/Gipsies at Home [20/65]
26 *Une Nuit terrible/A Terrible Night [20/65]
27 Déchargement de Bateaux (Le Havre)/Unloading the Boat (Havre) [20/65]
28 Plage de Villiers par gros temps/The Beach at Villiers in a Gale (May–June) [20/65]
29 Les Quais à Marseilles/The Docks at Marseilles [20/65]
30 Jetée et Plage de Trouville (1er partie)/Beach and Pier at Trouville (Part One) [20/65]
31 Barque sortant du port de Trouville/Boat Leaving the Harbour of Trouville [20/65]
32 Jetée et Plage de Trouville (2e partie)/Beach and Pier at Trouville Part Two [20/65]
33 Jour de marché à Trouville/Market Day (Trouville) [20/65]
34 Panorama du Havre (pris d'un bateau)/Panorama of Havre Taken From a Boat [20/65]
35 Arrivée d'un Train (Gare de Joinville)/Arrival of a Train (Joinville Station) [20/65]
36 Salut malencontreux d'un déserteur/A Soldier's Unlucky Salutation [20/65]
37 Dessinateur express (M. Thiers)/A Lightning Sketch (Mr Thiers) [20/65]
38 Les Forgerons/Blacksmith in His Workshop [20/65]
39 Tribulations d'un Concierge/A Janitor in Trouble [20/65]
40 Baignade en mer/Sea Bathing [20/65]
41 Enfants jouant sur la plage/Children Playing on the Beach [20/65]
42 Dix chapeaux en 60 secondes/Conjuror Making Ten Hats in Sixty Seconds [20/65]
43 Effets de mer sur les rochers/Sea Breaking on the Rocks [20/65]
44 Danse Serpentine/A Serpentine Dance [20/65]
45 Miss de Vère/Miss de Vère (English Jig) [20/65]
46 Départ des Automobiles/Automobiles Starting on a Race [20/65]
47 Revue navale à Cherbourg/A Naval Review at Cherbourg [20/65]
48 Cortège de Tzar allant à Versailles/The Czar and His Cortège Going to Versailles (September) [20/65]
49 Les Haleurs de Bateaux/Towing a Boat on the River [20/65]
50 Cortège de Tzar au Bois de Boulogne/The Czar's Cortège in the Bois de Boulogne [20/65]
51 Sortie des Ateliers Vibert/Closing Hours at Vibert's Perfume Factory [20/65]
52 La Voiture du Potier/The Potter's Cart [20/65]
53 Le Papier Protée/The Mysterious Paper [20/65]
54 Place de la Concorde/ditto [20/65]
55 La Gare Saint-Lazare/St Lazare Railroad Station [20/65]
56 Grandes Manœuvres/Manœuvres of the French Army [20/65]
57 Dessinateur: Chamberlain/A Lightning Sketch (Chamberlain) [20/65]
58 Place de la Bastille/ditto [20/65]
59 Marée montante sur brise-larmes/Tide Rising Over the Breakwater [20/65]
60 Retour au cantonnement/Return to the Barracks [20/65]
61 Dessinateur: Reine Victoria/A Lightning Sketch (H.M. Queen Victoria) [20/65]

62 Réunion d'Officiers/French Officers' Meeting [20/65]
63 Tempête sur la Jetée du Tréport/The Pier at Tréport During a Storm [20/65]
64 Le Bivouac/The Bivouac [20/65]
65 Batteuse à vapeur/Threshing-Machines Worked by Power [20/65]
66 Sac au dos/Sacks Up! [20/65]
67 Libération des territoriaux/Breaking up of the Territorial Army (France) [20/65]
68 Départ des Officiers/Officers of French Army Leaving Service [20/65]
69 Place Saint-Augustin/ditto [20/65]
70 *Escamotage d'une Dame chez Robert-Houdin/The Vanishing Lady (October–November) [20/65]
71 Le Fakir, mystère Indien/The Fakir (a Hindoo Mystery) [20/65]
72 L'Hôtel empoisonné/A Badly Managed Hotel [20/65]
73 Dessinateur: Von Bismark/A Lightning Sketch (Von Bismark) [20/65]
74 Les Indiscrets/The Peeping Toms [20/65]
75 Tom Old Boot/Tom Old Boot (a grotesque dwarf) [20/65]
76 Une altercation au café/A Quarrel in a Café [20/65]
77 Les Ivrognes/The Drunkards [20/65]
78–80 Le Manoir du Diable/The Devil's Castle/The Haunted Castle [60/195]

1897
81 Chicot, Dentiste américain/An Up-to-Date Dentist [20/65]
82 Le Cauchemar/A Nightmare [20/65]
83–84 Le Cortège du Bœuf Gras passant Place de la Concorde/The Mardi Gras Procession [40/130]
85 Cortège du Bœuf Gras boulevard des Italiens/The Mardi Gras Procession [20/65]
86 Une Cour de Ferme/A Farm Yard [20/65]
87 Les Apprentis Militaires/Military Apprentices [20/65]
88 Paulus chantant: Derrière l'Omnibus/Comedian Paulus Singing "Derrière l'Omnibus" [20/65]
89 Paulus chantant: Coquin de Printemps/Comedian Paulus Singing "Coquin de Printemps" [20/65]
90 Paulus chantant: Duelliste marseillais/Comedian Paulus Singing "Duelliste Marseillais" [20/65]
— Paulus chantant: Père la Victoire (hors catalogue) [20/65]
— Paulus chantant: En revenant d'la revue (hors catalogue) [20/65]
91 Défilé des Pompiers/Firemen on Parade [20/65]
92 Danseuses au Jardin de Paris/Dancing Girls (Jardin de Paris) [20/65]
93 Le Malade imaginaire/An Imaginary Patient (May) [20/65]
94 Le Musulman rigolo/A Funny Mahometan [20/65]
95 L'Hallucination de l'Alchimiste/An Hallucinated Alchemist [20/65]
96 Le Château hanté/The Haunted Castle/The Devil's Castle [20/65]
97–98 Cortège de la Mi-Carême/Mid-Lent Process in Paris [40/130]
99 Bataille de confettis/Battle with Confetti [20/65]
100 Sur les toits/On the Roofs [20/65]
101 D. Devant (Prestidigitateur)/D. Devant, Conjuror [20/65]
102 L'École des Gendres/The School for Sons-in-law [20/65]
103–104 Épisodes de Guerre/War Episodes (June) [40/130]

105 Les Dernières Cartouches/The Last Cartridges [20/65]
106 La Prise de Tournavos/The Surrender of Tournavos [20/65]
107 Exécution d'un Espion/Execution of a Spy [20/65]
108 Massacres en Crète/Massacre in Crete [20/65]
109 Passage dangereux, Mont Blanc/A Dangerous Pass (Mont Blanc) [20/65]
110 Combat naval en Grèce/Sea Fighting in Greece [20/65]
111 Gugusse et l'Automate/Gugusse and the Automaton [20/65]
112 *Entre Calais et Douvres/Between Calais and Dover [20/65]
113 L'Indiscret aux Bains de mer/Peeping Tom at the Seaside [20/65]
114 Dans les Coulisses/Behind the Scenes [20/65]
115 Tourneur en Poterie/A Potterymaker [20/65]
116 La Cigale et la Fourmi/The Grasshopper and the Ant [20/65]
117 Ascension d'un Ballon/A Balloon Ascension [20/65]
118–120 Le Cabinet de Mephistophélès/Laboratory of Mephistopheles [60/195]
121 Figaro et l'Auvergnat/The Barber and the Farmer [20/65]
122–123 *L'Auberge ensorcelée/The Bewitched Inn [40/130]
124 Auguste et Bibb/Auguste and Bibb [20/65]
125 Chirurgien américain/A Twentieth Century Surgeon [20/65]
126 Arlequin et Charbonnier/The Charcoal Man's Reception [20/65]
127 En Cabinet particulier/A Private Dinner [20/65]
128 *Après le Bal (le Tub)/After the Ball [20/65]
129 Le Magnétiseur/A Hypnotist at Work/While Under a Hypnotist's Influence [20/65]
130–131 Le Modèle irascible/An Irritable Model [40/130]
132 Danse au Sérail/Dancing in a Harem [20/65]
133 Vente d'Esclaves au Harem/Slave Trading in a Harem [20/65]
134 Combat dans une rue aux Indes/Fighting in the Streets in India [20/65]
135 Attaque d'une Poste anglais/Attack on an English Blockhouse [20/65]
136 Match de Boxe (École de Joinville)/Boxing Match [20/65]
137 Vision d'Ivrogne/A Drunkard's Dream [20/65]
138 *Faust et Marguérite/Faust and Marguerite [20/65]

1898

139 Carrefour de l'Opéra/Place de l'Opéra, 3rd View [20/65]
140–141 Magie Diabolique/Black Art/Devilish Magic [40/130]
142 Les Rayons X/A Novice at X-Rays [20/65]
143 Collision et Naufrage en mer/Collision and Shipwreck at Sea [20/65]
144–145 Quais de la Havane/The Blowing up of the *Maine* in Havana Harbour [40/130]
146 Visite de l'épave du *Maine*/A View of the Wreck of the *Maine* [20/65]
147 *Visite sous-marin du *Maine*/Divers at Work on the Wreck of the *Maine*/Divers at Work on a Wreck Under Sea [20/65]
148 Assaut d'escrime (École de Joinville)/Fencing at the Joinville School [20/65]
149 Le Maçon maladroit/A Clumsy Mason [20/65]
150 Combat naval devant Manille/Defending the Fort at Manila [20/65]

151 *Panorama pris d'un train en marche/Panorama from Top of Moving Train [20/65]

152 Corvée de Quartier accidentée/A Soldier's Tedious Duty [20/65]

153 *Le Magicien/The Magician/Black Magic [20/65]

154 Sorti sans Permission/A Soldier's French Leave [20/65]

155 *Illusions Fantasmagoriques/The Famous Box Trick [20/65]

156 Pygmalion et Galathée/Pygmalion and Galatea [20/65]

157 Montagnes Russes nautiques/Shooting the Chutes [20/65]

158 *Damnation de Faust/Damnation of Faust [20/65]

159 Guillaume Tell et le Clown/Adventures of William Tell [20/65]

160–162 *La Lune à un mètre/L'Homme dans la Lune/The Astronomer's Dream, or the Man in the Moon [60/195]

163 Prenez garde à la peinture/Fresh Paint [20/65]

164 La Caverne maudite/The Cave of the Demons [20/65]

165 Rêve d'artiste/The Artist's Dream [20/65]

166 Atelier d'Artiste, farce de Modèles/The Painter's Studio [20/65]

167 *Un Homme de tête/The Four Troublesome Heads [20/65]

168 Dédoublement cabalistique/The Triple Lady [20/65]

169 *Tentation de saint Antoine/Temptation of Saint Anthony [20/65]

170 Rêve du Pauvre/The Beggar's Dream [20/65]

171 *Salle à manger fantastique/A Dinner Under Difficulties [20/65]

172 Créations spontanées/Illusions fantastiques/Fantastical Illusions [20/65]

1899

173–174 Funérailles de Félix Faure/Funeral of Felix Faure (February) [40/130]

175–176 Cléopâtre/Robbing Cleopatra's Tomb [40/130]

177–178 Le Coucher de la Mariée ou Triste Nuit de Noce/The Bridegroom's Dilemma [40/130]

179 Duel politique/A Political Duel [20/65]

180 Luttes extravagantes/An Extraordinary Wrestling Match [20/65]

181 Richesse et Misère ou La Cigale et la Fourmi/The Wandering Minstrel [20/65]

182 L'Ours et la Sentinelle/The Sentry's Stratagem [20/65]

183 *L'Impressioniste fin de siècle/Illusioniste fin de siècle/An Up-to-Date Conjuror [20/65]

184 Le Spectre/Murder Will Out [20/65]

185–187 Le Diable au Couvent/The Devil in A Convent/The Sign of the Cross [60/195]

188 La Danse du Feu/Haggard's "She"—The Pillar of Fire [20/65]

189 La Crémation/The Spanish Inquisition [20/65]

190 Un bon lit/A Midnight Episode [20/65]

191 Force doit rester à la Loi/The slippery Burglar [20/65]

192 Pick-pocket et Policeman/A Drop Too Much [20/65]

193 Combat de Coqs/A Lively Cock-Fight [20/65]

194–195 Automaboulisme et Autorité/The Clown and Automobile/The Clown and Motor Car [40/130]

196 *Le Portrait mystérieux/A Mysterious Portrait [20/65]

197 Le Conférencier distrait/Absent-minded Lecturer [20/65]

198 La Pierre philosophale/The Philosopher's Stone [20/65]

199 Le Miroir de Cagliostro/Cagliostro's Mirror [20/65]

200 Neptune et Amphitrite/Neptune and Amphitrite [20/65]

201 Panorama du Port de St-Hélier/Bird's-Eye View of St Helier (Jersey) [20/65]

202 Entrée d'un Paquebot, Port de Jersey/Steamer Entering the Harbour of Jersey [20/65]

203 Débarquement de Voyageurs, Port de Granville/Passengers Landing at Harbour of Granville [20/65]

204 Le Christ marchant sur les flots/Christ Walking on the Water [20/65]

205 Évocation spirite/Summoning the Spirits [20/65]

206–217 *L'Affaire Dreyfus/The Dreyfus Affair/Dreyfus Court Martial (September) [240/780]

218 La Pyramide de Triboulet/The Human Pyramid [20/65]

219–224 *Cendrillon/Cinderella (October) [120/410]

225 La Statue de Neige/The Snow Man [20/65]

226–227 Le Chevalier Mystère/The Mysterious Knight [40/130]

228–229 L'Homme Protée/The Lightning Change Artist/The Chameleon Man [40/130]

230–231 Charmant voyages de Noces/The Interrupted Honeymoon [40/130]

1900

232–233 Panorama de la Seine/Panorama of River Seine [40/130]

234 Tom Whisky ou l'Illusioniste toqué/Addition and Subtraction [20/65]

235 Fatale méprise/The Railroad Pickpocket/The Railway Pickpocket [20/65]

236 Un Intrus dans une loge de Figurantes/An Intruder Behind the Scenes [20/65]

237–240 Les Miracles du Brahmane/The Miracles of Brahmin [80/260]

241 Farces de Marmitons/Scullion's Joke on the Chef [20/65]

242 Les Trois Bacchantes/The Three Bacchants [20/65]

243 La Vengeance du Gâte-Sauce/The Cook's Revenge [20/65]

244 Les Infortunes d'un Explorateur/The Misfortunes of an Explorer [20/65]

245–261 Exposition de 1900/Paris Exposition, 1900 [540/1105]

262–263 *L'Homme Orchestre/The One-Man Band [40/130]

264–275 Jeanne d'Arc/Joan of Arc [250/815]

276–278 Les Sept Péchés capitaux/The Seven Capital Sins [60/195]

279 Le Prisonnier récalcitrant/The Tricky Prisoner [20/65]

280 UNIDENTIFIED FILM

281–282 La Rêve du Rajah ou la Forêt enchantée/The Rajah's Dream or the Bewitched Wood [50/165]

283 Les Deux Aveugles/The Two Blind Men [25/82]

284 L'Artiste et le Mannequin/The Artist and the Manikin [25/82]

285–286 Le Sorcier, le Prince et le bon Génie/The Wizard, the Prince and the Good Fairy/The Sorcerer, the Prince and the Good Fairy [40/130]

287 Ne bougeons plus!/Don't Move [20/65]

288 Le Fou assassin/The Dangerous Lunatic [25/82]

289–291 Le Livre magique/The Magic Book [60/195]

292 Vue de Remerciements au Public/Thanking the Audience [30/100]

293 Spiritisme abracadabrant/Up-to-Date Spiritualism [20/65]

294 L'Illusioniste double et la Tête vivante/The Triple Conjuror and the Living Head [26/85]

295–297 Le Songe d'or de l'Avare/The Miser's Dream of Gold/The Miser or the Gold Country [70/230]

298–305 *Le Rêve de Noël/The Christmas Dream [160/520]

306 Gens qui pleurent et Gens qui rient/Crying and Laughing [20/65]

307–308 Coppélia ou la Poupée animée/Coppelia, the Animated Doll [40/130]

309–310 *Nouvelles Luttes extravagantes/Fat and Lean Wrestling Match/The Wrestling Sextette [50/165]

311 Le Repas fantastique/A Fantastical Meal [30/100]

312–313 Le Déshabillage impossible/Going to Bed Under Difficulties/An Increasing Wardrobe [40/130]

314 Le Tonneau des Danaïdes/The Danaids' Barrel/Eight Girls in a Barrel [25/82]

315 Le Malade hydrophobe/The Man With Wheels in His Head/The Gouty Patient [20/65]

1901

316 Une Mauvaise Plaisanterie/Practical Joke in a Bar Room [20/65]

317 Le Savant et le Chimpanzé/The Doctor and the Monkey [20/65]

318–319 L'Homme aux cent trucs/The Conjuror With A Hundred Tricks [50/165]

320–321 Guguste et Belzebuth/The Clown Versus Satan [40/130]

322 Le Reveil d'un Monsieur pressé/How He Missed His Train [20/65]

323–324 La Chirurgie de l'Avenir/Twentieth Century Surgery [40/130]

325–326 La Maison tranquille/What Is Home Without the Boarder? [40/130]

327 La Congrès des Nations en Chine/China Versus Allied Powers (August) [25/82]

328 Mésaventures d'un Aéronaute/The Balloonist's Mishap [20/65]

329–331 La Tour maudite/The Bewitched Dungeon [60/195]

332–333 *La Chrysalide et le Papillon d'or/Le Brahmane et le Papillon/The Brahmin and the Butterfly [40/130]

334 Bouquet d'illusions/The Triple-Headed Lady [20/65]

335–336 *Dislocation mystèrieuse/Dislocation Extraordinary [40/130]

337–344 Le Petit Chaperon Rouge/Little Red Riding Hood [160/520]

345–347 L'Antre des Esprits/The Magician's Cavern/The House of Mystery [60/195]

348–349 Le Chimiste repopulateur/A Maiden's Paradise [50/165]

350–351 Chez la Sorcière/The Bachelor's Paradise [40/130]

352–353 Le Temple de la Magie/The Temple of the Sun [40/130]

354 Le Charlatan/Painless Dentistry [20/65]

355 Une Noce au Village/Fun in Court/Contempt of Court [20/65]

356 Le Chevalier démontable et le Général Boum/A Good Trick/The Fierce Charger and the Knight [20/65]

357–358 Excelsior!/ditto/The Prince of Magicians [40/130]

359 L'Omnibus des toqués/Échappés de Charenton/Off to Bloomingdale Asylum/Off to Bedlam [20/65]

360 La Fontaine sacrée ou la Vengeance de Boudha/The Sacred Fountain [30/100]

361–370 *Barbe-Bleue/Blue Beard [210/690]

371–372 Le Chapeau à surprises/The Hat With Many Surprises [50/165]

373 La Phrénologie burlesque/A Phrenological Burlesque/The Phrenologist and the Lively Skull [30/100]

374-375 La Libellule/The Dragon Fly [40/130]
376-378 L'École infernale/The Trials of a Schoolmaster [60/195]

1902

379-380 Le Rêve du Pariah/The Dream of a Hindu Beggar [40/130]
381 Le Bataillon élastique/The Elastic Batallion [20/65]
382-383 *L'Homme à la tête de Caoutchouc/The Man With the Rubber Head/A Swelled Head [50/165]
384-385 Le Diable géant ou le miracle de la Madonne/The Devil and the Statue/The Gigantic Devil [40/130]
386 Nain et Géant/The Dwarf and the Giant/The Long and Short of It [20/65]
387-389 L'Armoire des Frères Davenport/The Cabinet Trick of the Davenport Brothers/The Mysterious Cabinet [65/212]
390 Les Piqueurs de Fûts/Wine Cellar Burglars/The Burglars in the Wine Cellar [30/100]
391 Douche du Colonel/The Colonel's Shower Bath/The Painter's Mishap in the Barracks [20/65]
392-393 L'Œuf du Sorcier/L'Œuf Magique Prolifique/Prolific Magical Egg/The Egg in Black Art [40/130]
394-396 La Danseuse microscopique/The Dancing Midget/Marvellous Egg Producing With Surprising Developments [60/195]
397 *Eruption volcanique à la Martinique/The Eruption of Mount Pelee/The Terrible Eruption of Mount Pelee and Destruction of St Pierre, Martinique (May) [30/100]
398 Catastrophe du Ballon "Le Pax"/The Catastrophe of the Balloon "Le Pax" (May) [20/65]
399-411 *Le Voyage dans la Lune/A Trip to the Moon (August) [260/845]
412 La Clownesse fantôme/The Shadow-girl/Twentieth Century Conjuring [30/100]
— *Le Sacré d'Édouard VII/The Coronation of Edward VII (hors catalogue) (August) [107/350]
413-414 *Les Trésors de Satan/The Treasures of Satan/The Devil's Money Bags [50/165]
415-416 L'Homme-Mouche/The Human Fly [40/130]
417-418 La Femme volante/Marvellous Suspension and Evolution [40/130]
419 L'Equilibre impossible/An Impossible Balancing Feat [25/82]
420-421 Le Pochard et l'Inventeur/Drunkard and Inventor/What Befell the Inventor's Visitor [50/165]
422-425 Une Indigestion/Chirurgie fin de siècle/Up-to-Date Surgery/Sure Cure For Indigestion [85/276]
426-429 Le Voyage de Gulliver à Lilliput et chez les Géants/Voyages de Gulliver/Gulliver's Travels Among the Lilliputians and the Giants [80/260]
430-443 Les Aventures de Robinson Crusoë/Robinson Crusoe [280/910]

1903

444 La Corbeille enchantée/The Enchanted Basket [25/82]
445-448 *La Guirlande merveilleuse/The Marvellous Wreath/The Marvellous Hoop [80/260]
449-450 Les Filles du Diable/Beelzebub's Daughters/The Women of Fire [50/165]

451–452 Un Malheur n'arrive jamais seul/Misfortune Never Comes Alone/Accidents Never Happen Singly [50/165]

453–457 Le Cake-walk infernal/The Cake Walk Infernal/The Infernal Cake Walk [100/325]

458–459 *La Boîte à malice/The Mysterious Box/The Shallow Box Trick [50/165]

460–461 Les Mousquetaires de la Reine/The Queen's Musketeers/The Musketeers of the Queen [50/165]

462–464 Le Puits fantastique/The Enchanted Well (June) [50/165]

465–469 *L'Auberge du Bon Repos/The Inn Where No Man Rests/The Inn of "Good Rest" (June) [105/345]

470–471 *La Statue animée/The Drawing Lesson, or the Living Statue (July) [48/160]

472 *La Flamme merveilleuse/The Mystical Flame (July) [37/120]

473–475 *Le Sorcier/The Witch's Revenge/The Sorcerer's Revenge (July) [67/220]

476 *L'Oracle de Delphes/The Oracle of Delphi (July) [30/100]

477–478 *Le Portrait spirite/A Spiritualistic Photographer (July) [44/145]

479–480 *Le Mélomane/The Melomaniac (June) [51/168]

481–482 *Le Monstre/The Monster (June) [51/168]

483–498 *Le Royaume des Fées/Fairyland, or The Kingdom of the Fairies/Wonders of the Deep (September) [320/1040]

499–500 *Le Chaudron infernal/The Infernal Cauldron and the Phantasmal Vapours (October) [36/116]

501–502 Le Revenant/The Apparition, or Mr Jones' Comical Experience With a Ghost/The Ghost and the Candle (October) [51/168]

503–505 *Le Tonnerre de Jupiter/Jupiter's Thunderbolts, or the Home of the Muses (October) [70/230]

506–507 *La Parapluie fantastique/Ten Ladies in One Umbrella/The Girls in One Umbrella (September) [56/185]

508–509 *Tom Tight et Dum Dum/Jack Jaggs and Dum Dum/The Rival Music Hall Artistes (September) [50/165]

510–511 *Bob Kick, l'Enfant terrible/Bob Kick the Mischievous Kid (November) [38/125]

512–513 *Illusions funambulesques/Extraordinary Illusions/The 20th Century Illustrationist (November) [41/135]

514–516 *L'Enchanteur Alcofrisbas/Alcofrisbas, the Master Magician/The Enchanter (November) [70/230]

517–519 *Jack et Jim/Jack and Jim/Comical Conjuring (December) [58/188]

520–524 *La Lanterne magique/The Magic Lantern (December) [97/315]

525–526 *Le Rêve du Maître de Ballet/The Ballet-Master's Dream/The Dream of the Ballet Master (December) [47/155]

527–533 *Faust aux Enfers/La Damnation de Faust/The Damnation of Faust/The Condemnation of Faust (December) [150/490]

1904

534–535 *Le Bourreau turc/The Terrible Turkish Executioner, or It Served Him Right (January) [45/150]

536–537 Les Apaches/A Burlesque Highway Robbery in "Gay Paree" [46/153]

538–539 *Au Clair de la Lune ou Pierrot malheureux/A Moonlight Serenade, or the Miser Punished (January) [57/187]

540–541 *Un Prêté pour un rendu/Une Bonne Farce avec ma tête/Tit for Tat, or a Good Joke With My Head (January) [39/128]

542–544 Match de Prestidigitation/A Wager Between Two Magicians, or "Jealous of Myself" [60/200]

545 Un Peu de feu, S. V. P./Every Man His Own Cigar Lighter [22/70]

546 Siva l'Invisible/The Invisible Silvia [29/95]

547–549 *Le Coffre enchanté/The Bewitched Trunk [68/224]

550–551 *Les Apparitions fugitives/The Fugitive Apparitions (February) [33/109]

552–553 *Le Roi du Maquillage/The Untamable Whiskers (February) [42/138]

554–555 *Le Rêve de l'Horloger/The Clockmaker's Dream (February) [51/168]

556–557 Les Transmutations imperceptibles/The Imperceptible Transmutations [38/124]

558–559 Un Miracle sous l'Inquisition/A Miracle Under the Inquisition [44/146]

560–561 Benvenuto Cellini ou une curieuse évasion/Benvenuto Cellini, or A Curious Evasion [53/176]

562–574 *Damnation du Doctor Faust/Faust and Marguerite/Faust (March) [261/850]

575–577 Le Joyeux Prophète russe/The Fake Russian Prophet [60/200]

578–580 Le Thaumaturge chinois/Tchin-Chao, the Chinese Conjuror [60/200]

581–584 *Le Merveilleux Éventail vivant/The Wonderful Living Fan [90/290]

585–588 *Sorcellerie culinaire/The Cook in Trouble (May) [84/275]

589–590 La Planche du Diable/The Devilish Plank [40/130]

591–592 *Le Dîner impossible/The Impossible Dinner [41/133]

593–595 *La Sirène/The Mermaid (May) [71/233]

596–597 Les Mésaventures de M. Boit-sans-Soif/The Mischances of a Drunkard [50/165]

598–602 La Providence de Notre-Dame des Flots/The Providence of the Waves, or the Dream of a Poor Fisherman [101/330]

603–605 La Fête au père Mathieu/Uncle Rube's Birthday [65/214]

606–625 Le Barbier de Seville/The Barber of Sevilla, or the Useless Precaution [412/1340] (the same shortened: 295/960)

626–627 Les Costumes animés/The Animated Costumes [50/165]

628–631 Les Invités de M. Latourte/Une Bonne Surprise/Simple Simon's Surprise Party [91/295]

632–633 Le Cadre aux surprises/The Astonishing Frame [40/130]

634–636 Le Rosier miraculeux/The Wonderful Rose-Tree [60/200]

637–638 La Dame fantôme/The Shadow Lady [53/176]

639–640 Mariage par correspondence/A Wedding by Correspondence [41/135]

641–661 *Le Voyage à travers l'Impossible/An Impossible Voyage/Whirling the Worlds [434/1410] (the same shortened: 378/1230)

662–664 Le Juif Errant/The Wandering Jew [60/200]

665–667 *Le Cascade de feu/The Firefall [60/200]

1905

668 La Grotte aux surprises/The Grotto of Surprises [38/125]

669–677 Détresse et Charité/The Christmas Angel/The Beggar Maiden [158/515]

678–679 Les Cartes vivantes/The Living Playing Cards [48/160]

680–682 Le Roi des Tireurs/The King of Sharpshooters [68/223]

683–685 Le Diable noir/The Black Imp [68/223]

686–689 Le Phénix ou le Coffret de cristal/The Crystal Casket [92/300]

690–692 Le Menuet lilliputien/The Lilliputian Minuet [60/200]

693–695 *Le Baquet de Mesmer/A Mesmerian Experiment [60/200]

696–698 Le Peintre Barbouillard et le Tableau diabolique/Mr Dauber and the Whimsical Picture [70/230]

699–701 Le Miroir de Venise. Une Mésaventure de Shylock/The Venetian Looking-glass [65/214]

702–704 Les Chevaliers du chloroforme/The Chloroform Fiends [67/220]

705–726 *Le Palais des Mille et Une Nuits/The Palace of the Arabian Nights [430/1400] (the same shortened: 338/1100)

727–731 Le Compositeur toqué/A Crazy Composer [103/335]

732–737 La Tour de Londres et les Dernières Moments d'Anne Boleyn/The Tower of London [103/335]

738–739 La Chaise à porteurs enchantée/The Enchanted Sedan Chair [56/185]

740–749 *Le Raid Paris–Monte Carlo en 2 heures/An Adventurous Automoible Trip [203/660]

750–752 L'Île de Calypso. Ulysse et le géant Polyphème/The Mysterious Island [69/226]

753–755 Un Feu d'artifice improvisé/Unexpected Fireworks [60/200]

756–775 *La Légende de Rip van Winkle/Rip's Dream (December) [335/1086]

776–779 Le Cauchemar du Pêcheur ou l'Escarpolette fantastique/The Angler's Nightmare, or a Policeman's Troubles [90/290]

780–783 Le Système du Docteur Sonflamort/Life-Saving Up-to-Date [93/304]

784–785 Le Tripot clandestin/The Scheming Gamblers' Paradise [54/180]

1906

786–788 Le Dirigeable fantastique ou le Cauchemar d'un Inventeur/The Inventor Crazybrains and his Wonderful Airship [60/200]

789–790 Une Chute de cinq étages/A Mix-up in the Gallery [55/183]

791–806 Jack le Ramoneur/The Chimney Sweep (March) [307/1000]

807–809 Le Maestro Do-mi-sol-do/Professor Do-mi-sol-do [69/225]

810–812 La Magie à travers les âges/Old and New Style Conjurors [74/240]

813–817 L'Honneur est satisfait/Who Looks, Pays! [108/350]

818–820 La Cardeuse de Matelas/The Tramp and the Mattress Makers [75/246]

821–823 Les Affiches en goguette/The Hilarious Posters (May) [60/200]

824–838 Les Incendiaires/Histoire d'un crime/A Desperate Crime [307/1000]

839–840 L'Anarchie chez Guignol/Punch and Judy [43/140]

841–843 Le Fantôme d'Alger/A Spiritualistic Meeting [76/250]

844–845 L'Hôtel des voyageurs de commerce/A Roadside Inn [70/230]
846–848 *Les Bulles de savon animées/Soap Bubbles (June) [70/230]
849–870 *Les 400 Farces du Diable/The Merry Frolics of Satan [323/1050]
871–873 Le Rastaquouère Rodriguez y Papanaguaz/A Seaside Flirtation [73/238]
874–876 L'Alchimiste Parafaragamus ou la Cornue infernale/The Mysterious Retort [60/200]
877–887 *La Fée carabosse ou le Poignard fatal/The Witch (November) [252/820]
888–905 Robert Macaire et Bertrand/Robert Macaire and Bertrand [325/1060]

1907
906–908 Le Carton fantastique/A Mischievous Sketch [74/243]
909–911 La Douche d'Eau bouillante/Rogues' Tricks [80/265]
912–924 Deux cent mille lieues sous les mers ou le cauchemar d'un pêcheur/Under the Seas [286/930]
925–928 Les Fromages automobiles/The Skipping Cheeses [85/280]
929–935 Le Mariage de Victorine/Le Mariage de Victoire/How Bridget's Lover Escaped [154/500]
936–950 *Le Tunnel sous la Manche ou le Cauchemar franco–anglais/Tunnelling the English Channel [307/1000]
951–955 La nouvelle peine de mort/A New Death Penalty (July) [123/400]
956–960 Le Delirium Tremens ou la fin d'un alcoolique/Drink! A Great Temperance Story [95/312]
961–968 L'Éclipse du soleil en pleine lune/The Eclipse [172/560]
969–973 Le Placard infernal/The Bewildering Cabinet (October) [114/370]
974–979 La Marche funèbre de Chopin/Chopin's Funeral March Burlesqued [140/460]
980–987 Hamlet/Hamlet, Prince of Denmark [175/570]
988–994 Bernard le Bûcheron ou le Miracle de saint Hubert/A Forester Made King [139/458]
995–999 Shakespeare. La Mort de Jules César/Shakespeare Writing "Julius Caesar" (November) [105/344]
1000–1004 *Pauvre John ou les Aventures d'un buveur de whiskey/Sight-seeing Through Whisky [108/353]
1005–1009 La Colle universelle/Good Glue Sticks [95/311]
1010–1013 Satan en prison/Satan in Prison [92/300]
1014–1017 *Ali Barbouyou et Ali Bouf à l'huile/Delirium in a Studio [93/302]
1018–1022 La Boulangerie modèle/Bakers in Trouble [112/365]

1908
1023–1029 La Perle des savants/An Angelic Servant [148/483]
1030–1034 *Le Tambourin fantastique/The Knight of Black Art (January) [114/371]
1035–1039 La Cuisine de l'ogre/In the Bogie Man's Cave (January) [107/350]
1040–1043 François 1er et Triboulet/The King and the Jester (January) [99/321]
1044–1049 Il y a un dieu pour les ivrognes/The Good Luck of a "Souse" (January) [137/445]

— Seek and Thou Shalt Find (January) [27/88]

1050–1065 Le Civilisation à travers les âges/Humanity Through the Ages (February) [307/1000]

1066–1068 Les Torches humaines/Justinian's Human Torches (February) [57/187]

1069–1072 La Génie du Feu/The Genii of Fire (February) [95/310]

1073–1080 Why That Actor Was Late [181/590]

1081–1085 Le Rêve d'un fumeur d'opium/The Dream of an Opium Fiend (March) [106/346]

1086–1090 Nuit de Carnaval/A Night With Masqueraders in Paris (March) [112/363]

1091–1095 La Photographie électrique à distance/Long Distance Wireless Photography (March) [113/366]

1096–1101 La Prophétesse de Thèbes/The Prophetess of Thebes (March) [139/458]

1102–1103 Salon de coiffure/In the Barber Shop (March) [55/180]

1104–1108 Quiproquo/A Mistaken Identity (April) [109/355]

1109–1113 Mariage de raison et mariage d'amour/A Lover's Hazing (April) [144/468]

1116–1123 L'Habit ne fait pas le moine/Le Fabricant de Diamants/A Fake-Diamond Swindler (April) [180/586]

1124–1131 La Curiosité puniée/Le Crime de la rue de Cherche-Midi à quatorze heures/Curiosity Punished (April) [173/564]

1132–1145 Le Nouveau Seigneur du Village [297/968]

1146–1158 L'Avare/The Miser (May) [270/877]

1159–1165 Le Conseil de pipelet/Up-to-Date Clothes Cleaning (?) (May) [143/465]

1166–1172 Le Serpent de la rue de la Lune/Pranks With a Fake Python (May) [153/497]

1173–1175 High Life Taylor/Sideshow Wrestlers (?) (May) [61/198]

1176–1185 Lulli ou le Violon brisé/The Broken Violin (June) [208/876]

1186–1189 Tartarin de Tarascon ou une chasse à l'ours/Hunting the Teddy Bear (June) [28/91]

1190 Le Trait d'Union/The Little Peacemaker (June) [34/110]

1191–1198 Rivalité d'amour/A Tragedy in Spain (June) [170/552]

Le Raid Paris–New York en automobile/Mishaps of the N.Y.–Paris Race (June) [380/1235]

On ne badine pas avec l'amour/No Trifling With Love (June) [length unknown]

Love and Molasses (July) [length unknown]

Mystery of the Garrison (July) [198/645]

Magic of Catchy Songs (July) [114/370]

Woes of Roller Skates (July) [139/453]

Le Fakir de Singapoure/Indian Sorcerer (July) [345/1121]

Le Jugement du Garde-Champêtre/The Forester's Remedy (?) (July) [167/543]

Mischances of a Photographer (July) [63/205]

Two Crazy Bugs (July) [172/560]

His First Job (August) [99/320]

French Interpreter Policeman/French Cops Learning English (August) [138/448]

At the Hotel Mix-Up (August) [154/500]

Oriental Black Art (August) [length unknown]

Tricky Painter's Fate (August) [73/237]

Two Talented Vagabonds (August) [123/400]

1314–1325 Conte de la Grand'mère et Rêve de l'Enfant/Au pays des Jouets/Grandmother's Story (September) [243/790]

Le Main secourable/Helping Hand (September) [75/245]

Buncoed Stage Johnnie (September) [81/263]

Not Guilty (September) [198/645]

Le Mariage de Thomas Poirot/Fun With the Bridal Party (September) [149/484]

Trop Vieux!/Old Footlight Favourite (?) (September) [181/588]

Anaïc ou le Balafré [192/624]

Pour l'étoile S. V. P. [77/250]

Pour les p'tiots [71/231]

La Fontaine merveilleuse [196/637]

L'Ascension de la rosière [128/416]

Voyage de noces en ballon/Honeymoon in a Balloon (October) [132/430]

Aventures de Don Quichotte/Incident From Don Quixote (October) [109/355]

Rude Awakening (October) [length unknown]

Wonderful Charm (October) [180/585]

The Duke's Good Joke (November) [286/930]

Pochardiana ou le rêveur éveillé [277/900]

La Toile d'araignée merveilleuse [103/335]

1372–1385 La Fée libellule/Le Lac enchanté [278/903]

1394–1407 La Génie des cloches/La Fête du sonneur [278/903]

Moitié de polka [177/575]

Hallucinations pharmaceutiques/La Truc du potard [260/845]

1429–1441 La bonne bergère et la méchante princesse [280/910]

La Poupée vivante [60/200]

1909

Cinderella Up-to-Date (October) [292/950]

For the Cause of Suffrage (October) [279/905]

Hypnotist's Revenge (November) [107/350]

For Sale—a Baby (November) [184/600]

A Tumultuous Elopement (November) [length unknown]

Count's Wooing (November) [153/497]

Mrs and Mr Duff (November) [150/488]

Fortune Favours the Brave (December) [186/608]

Seein' Things (December) [87/286]

1910

1476–1486 *Hydrothérapie fantastique [240/780]

Le Traitment 706/Guérison de l'obésité en 5 minutes (September?) [124/403]

1495–1501 *Le Locataire diabolique [120/390]

1502–1507 Un Homme comme il faut [120/390]

1508–1512 Les Illusions fantaisistes [100/325]

1513–1521 Si j'étais le roi!!! (October?) [180/585]

1522–1529 Le Roi des Médiums/Apparitions fantômatiques (October?) [167/543]

1530–1533 Le Papillon fantastique [80/260]

La Gigue merveilleuse [40/130]

Le Mousquetaire de la Reine [length unknown]
Le Conte du vieux Talute [length unknown]
Les sept barres d'or [300/975]
Galatée [length unknown]
L'Homme aux mille inventions [length unknown]
Le Secret du Médécin/The Doctor's Secret [229/743]

1911

*Les Hallucinations du Baron de Münchausen (September) [235/764]
Le Vitrail diabolique [length unknown]

1912

*À la Conquête du Pôle/Conquest of the Pole (February) [650/2112]
*Cendrillon ou la pantoufle mystérieuse/Cinderella, or the Glass Slipper (October) [615/2000]
*Le Chevalier des Neiges (November) [400/1300]
Le Voyage de la Famille Bourrichon [405/1316]

Appendix IV

GASTON MÉLIÈS FILMOGRAPHY

This filmography was prepared by consulting the following sources:

Star Film Catalogue, 1903–8.
The Moving Picture World, 1909–12.
Enciclopedia dello Spettacolo, vol. VII, Unione Editoriale, Rome, 1960.

Where appropriate, the format follows that of the *Georges Méliès Filmography*.

1903
482A Une Course de yachts/The Yacht Race (Reliance–Shamrock III) (August) [43/140]

1905
668A Inauguration Subjects: President-Elect Roosevelt, Vice-President-Elect Fairbanks and Escort Going to the Capitol (February) [45/146]

1908
1114–1115 The Catholic Centennial Celebration (May) [292/950] Pageant, Dedication, Festival/Boston Normal School Pageant (June) [length unknown]

1909
The Stolen Wireless (October) [289/915]
The Red Star Inn (November) [307/1000]
The Fatal Ball (December) [307/1000]

1910–12
(One-reelers made in Texas and California between April 7 1910 and July 25 1912)

Cyclone Pete in Matrimony
Making Sherry Wine at Xeres
Branding the Thief
The Seal of the Church
The First Born
The Lovers' Oracle
Trawlers Fishing in a Hurricane
The Story of Old Mexico
Volcanic Eruptions
The Rival Miners
The Debt Repaid
Indian Drama
Speed Versus Death
A Thrilling Race Against Time
A Race for a Bride
A Rough Night on the Bridge
The Palefaced Princess
The Padre's Secret

Love's C. Q. D.
A Texas Joke
White Doe's Lovers
The Stranded Actor
The Ruling Passion
The Little Preacher
The Golden Secret
A Postal Substitute
The Woman in the Case
Mrs Bargainday's Baby
The Return to To-Wa-Wa
The Winning Way
The Romance of Circle Ranch
Won in the Fifth
In the Mission Shadows
The Salt on the Bird's Tail
A Plucky American Girl
Bill's Sister Baseball That's All

Out of Mischief
Uncle Jim
Under the Stars and Bars
Birthday Cigars
Generous Customers
A Mountain Wife
His Sergeant's Stripes
The Cowboy and the Bachelor
   Girl
Pals
What Great Bear Learned
Old Norris' Gal
A Western Welcome
In the Tall Grass Country
The Crimson Scars
The Owner of the 'LL' Ranch
Changing Cooks
How Mary Met the Cowpunchers
Only a Sister
Tony the Greaser
Billy and his Pal
My Prairie Flower
In the Hot Lands
The Snake in the Grass
The Schoolmarm of Coyote
   County
Sir Percy and the Punchers
The Warrant for Red Rube
Her Faithful Heart
Jack Wilson's Last Deal
An Unwilling Cowboy
The Reformation of Jack Robins
Mary's Stratagem
The Spring Round-Up
The Redemption of Rawhide
The Immortal Alamo
In Time for Press
Her Spoiled Boy
When the Tables Turned
The Kiss of Mary Jane
The Honor of the Flag
Right of Way
The Great Heart of the West
The Strike at the Gringo
Bessie's Ride
At the Gringo Mine
Red Cloud's Secret
His Terrible Lesson
The Local Bully
Two Foolies and their Follies
A Spanish Love Song

The Call of the Wilderness
A Shattered Dream
$200.00
The Mission Waif
The Hobo Cowboy
The Stolen Grey
Tommy's Rocking Horse
The Cross of Pearls
The Gypsy Bride
Right or Wrong
Mexican As It Is Spoken
The Spur of Necessity
The Miser Miner
An Oil County Romance
The Reason Why
A Western Girl
The Better Man
The Mission Father
The Ranch Man's Debt of
   Honour
A Woman's Gratitude
Roped In
Alice's Choice
The Outlaw and the Baby
The Mortgage
Cowboy Vs Tenderfoot
Dodging the Sheriff
Smiling Bob
Melita's Ruse
The Swastika
All Is Fair
The Rustler's Daughter
Oil
The Sheriff's Daughter
Troubles of the XL Outfit
The Remittance Man
A Man Worth While
Wanted–A Wife
The Ghost of Sulphur
   Mountain
True Till Death
A Cowboy's Proposal
Finding the 'Last Chance' Mine
Widowers Three
Making Good
Ghosts at Circle X Camp
Two Loves
A Woman's Way
The Cowboy Kid
The Man Inside
A String of Beads

1912–13   *Gaston Méliès*
(Films made during a voyage across the Pacific to south-east Asia   *Filmography*
  between July 1912 and May 1913)   [151]

The Misfortunes of Mr and Mrs
  Mott on Their Trip to Tahiti
A Tale of Old Tahiti
Unmasked by a Kanaka
A Ballad of the South Seas
The Upa Upa Dance
The River Wanganui
A Tahitian Fish Drive
How Chief Te Ponga Won His
  Bride
Loved by a Maori Chief
Captured by Boomerang
  Throwers
The Golden Gullen
The Black Trackers
The Foster Brothers
Gold and the Gilded Way
The Stolen Claim

The Lure of the Sacred Pearl
It Happened in Java
Javanese Dancers
Snapshots of Java
Views of Samarang
Native Industries of Java
The Robber of Angkor
A Cambodian Idyll
Lost in Cambodia
The Poisoned Darts
His Chinese Friend
A Chinese Funeral
The Yellow Slave
The Rice Industry in Japan
Temples of Japan
A Japanese Wedding
Japanese Judo Commonly
  Known as Jiu Jitsu

(Entries in italics refer to films, tricks, stage spectaculars, paintings, books or magazines.
Page numbers in italics refer to illustrations.)

Abbey, Edwin Austin (painter), 53
Académie de Prestidigitation, 58
Adventures of William Tell, The, 90
Adventurous Automobile Trip, An, 60, 114, *115*, *117*, 120, *125*
Afternoon Wind (painting), *107*
After the Ball, 33, 113, *113*
Alcofrisbas the Enchanter (stage production), 102
Alcofrisbas, the Master Magician, 100
Alcy, Jehanne d' (otherwise known as Charlotte-Stéphanie Faes and Fanny Manieux), 22, 30, 33, *45*, 82, 110, 111, *113*
Alhambra (London), 53, 60
Alhambra (Paris), 72
Allotte de la Fuÿe, Marguérite (writer), 119
Amateur Singer, The (operetta), 81
American Kinema, 55
American Mutoscope and Biograph Company, 17, 48
American Spiritualistic Mediums, or The Recalcitrant Decapitated Man (stage production), 16, 23, *24*, 102
American Wildwest, 74
Andersen, Hans Christian, 108
André, Victor (actor), 51
Animatographe, 28, *28*
Antonio Davolio, the Trapezist (automaton), 19, *19*
Apollinaire, Guillaume, 92
Apparition, or Mr. Jones' Comical Experience With a Ghost, The, 56
Arcana (stage production), *111*
Armand-Fix, Pierre (artiste), 81
Arnould (conjuror), 22
Around the World in Eighty Days (pantomime), 22
Around the World in Eighty Days (novel), 120
Arrival of a Train in Vincennes Station, 117
Arrival of a Train (Joinville Station), 29
Arroseur arrosé, L', 29
Artist's Dream, The (illusion), 90
Association International des Fabricants de Films, 66
Astaix (worker), 44, 55
Astronomer's Dream, or The Man In the Moon, The, 36
At the Hotel Mix-Up, 124
Aurenche, Jean (producer), 85
Auriol, J.-G., 83
Automobile Starting on a Race, 117
Awakening of Chrysis, The, 112

Bachelard, Gaston, 104, 125
Bain turc, Le (painting), 112

Bairal, Mlle (actress), 113
Ballet-Master's Dream, The, 57
Barnum and Bailey, 98n
Barber, The (silhouette), 26
Barber of Sevilla, The, 58, *58*
Baron Münchausen, 85
Baudelaire, Charles, 13
Beach at Villiers in a Gale, The, 29
Beast With Five Fingers, The, 103
Beaumarchais, 58
Beautiful Season, The (frottage), 62, *62*
Beelzebub's Daughters, or The Women of Fire, 111
Berlioz, 57
Bernon, Bluette (actress), *45*, 53, *109*
Bessy, Maurice (historian), 10
Bewitched Inn, The, 124
Biograph Company, 67
Bioscope, 96
Black Maria, 31
Bleeding Nun (stage production), 38
Blet, Charlotte (artiste), 81
Blue Beard, 45, *45*, 59n
Boat Leaving the Harbour at Trouville, 117
Bobinos (Parisian theatre), 112
Booth, Walter R. (director), 51, 94, 94n
Botticelli, 108
Boulanger, General, 26, 27, *27*
Boulevard du Cinéma à l'époque de Georges Méliès, Le (book), 10
Bracken (cameraman), 76, *76*
Bracken, Mildred (actress), 74, 76
Brady, Jeanne (actress), 33, *113*
Brahmin and the Butterfly, The, 104, *105*
Brakhage, Stan, 8
Branding the Thief, 74
Breton, André, 7, 9
Bridegroom's Dilemma, The, 40
Brunnet (actor), 53
Brutal Explosion (silhouette), 26
Buffalo Bill Show, 74
Buñuel, Luis, 59, 103
Burckhardt, Rudy, *52*
Burlesque Waxworks, The (lantern slides), 26

Cabinet Trick of the Davenport Brothers, The, 17, *17*
Cago, De (conjuror), 59
Calmels, Eugène (mechanic), 19
Cambodian Idyll, A, *76*

Carmelli (conjuror), 22, 42
Carné, Marcel, 85
Caroly (conjuror), 59
Carroll, Lewis, 91, 120
Catalepsy and the Cops (stage production), 23
Catastrophe of the Balloon 'Pax', 51
Cave of the Demons, The, 37
Chambre Syndicale de la Prestidigitation, 58, *58*, 70, 81, 84, 85
Chambre Syndicale des Éditeurs Cinématographiques, 42, 58, 66
Chambre Syndicale Française de la Cinématographie, 83
Chaplin, Charlie, 97, 97n
Charles Urban Trading Company, 53, 94n
Châtelet (Parisian theatre), 22, 44, 53, 62, 64, 102
Cheat, The, 83
Chélu, Caroline (artiste), 22
Chevalier des neiges, Le, 80
Chien Andalou, Un, 103
Chimney Sweep, The, 61, *109*, 113, 122, 124
Chinese Shadows (silhouettes), 26
Chirico, Giorgio de, 87n
Chocolat Meunier, 97
Christ Walking on the Water, 40
Christmas Angel, The, 59, *60*
Christmas Dream, The, 44
Cinderella (pantomime), 22, 33
Cinderella, 42, *43*, 59n
Cinderella, or The Glass Slipper, 79, *79*, 79n, 80
Cinderella Up-to-Date, 72
Ciné-Actualités (Parisian cinema), 81
Ciné-Journal (magazine), 82, 83
Cinématographe, 28, *28*, 33, 95
Ciné-Salon (Parisian cinema), 81
Claudel (scenery-painter), 47
Clément-Maurice (businessman), 70
Clifford, William (actor), 74
Close Up (magazine), 83
Cocoon, The (illusion), 108
Cohl, Émile, 40, 56
College of 'Pataphysics, 58
Comédie Française, 44
Comfortable Inn, A, 26
Condemnation of Faust, The (otherwise known as *The Damnation of Faust*), 57, 58
Conjuring, 29
Conquest of the Pole, The, 79, *80*
Conservatoire Nationale des Arts et Métiers, 83
Cooke, George Alfred, 15, 16, 108
Cook In Trouble, The, 58

Cook's Revenge, The, 42
Coquelin aîné (actor), 14
Coquelin cadet (actor), 18
Coronation of Edward VII, The, 53, *55*
Cottens, Victor de (writer), 60, 62, 115
Coty (perfumier), 83
Coussy, Mme (guardian of Eugénie Génin), 18
Couture, Thomas (painter), 112
Cowboy Kid, The, 74, *75*
Cranach, Lucas, 108, *109*
Crazy Composer, A, 60
Criterion Theatre (Chicago), 67
Curiosity Punished, 68
Cyclone Pete In Matrimony, 74
Czar and his Cortège Going to Versailles, 34

Dali, Salvador, 103
Dancing Midget, The, 50
Darlay, Victor (musician), 62
Darwin, Charles, 17
Davenport Brothers (actors), 16, 101, 102, 103
David, Jules (otherwise known as Marius, an artiste), 22, 23, 81
D. Devant, Conjuror, 33
Debrie, André (mechanic), 31
Dedi of Dedsnefru (conjuror), 101
Deed, André (otherwise known as Cretinetti, Gribouille, Glupishkin and Foolshead), 103
Delannoy, Henri (actor), 51
Delion Hats, 35
Delirium In a Studio, 67
Demenÿ, Georges (inventor), 33
De Mille, Cecil B., 83
Deslandes, Jacques (historian), 10, 59n
Desperate Crime, A, 61, *61*
Devant, David (conjuror), 17, 37, 90, *94*
Devil and the Statue, The, 49, *49*
Devil in A Convent, The, 112
Devil's Castle, The, 30
Dewar's Whiskey, 35
Dircks, Henry (engineer), 38
Dislocation Extraordinary, 96, 102
Disney, Walt, 40, *41*
Disraeli, Benjamin, 17
Divers At Work on the Wreck of the 'Maine', 36, 55
Donaldson Lithographing Company, 62, 62n
Donnay, Maurice (dramatist), 14
Doublier (cameraman), 29
Dounie, James M. (business manager), 66, 66n
Downey, F. (exhibitor), 66n
Downey, J. (exhibitor), 66n

Dreyfus Affair, The, 42
Dreyfus, Alfred, 27, 42, 95
Druhot, Léon (cinéaste), 83
Duck Soup, 123
Dufayel, M (businessman), 83
Duperrey (conjuror), 22
Dwarf and the Giant, The, 49, 97

Eastman, George, 69
Eastman Kodak Company, 28, 67
Éclair Company, 66, 70, 72
Eclipse, The, 64, 65, 113
École des Beaux-Arts (Paris), 17
Edison, Thomas A., 28, 31, 34, 66, 67, 71
Egyptian Hall (magic theatre in London), 15, 15, 17, 108
Eilshemius, Louis (painter), 106, 107
Elastic Battalion, The, 50
Eliade, Mircea, 108
Enchanted Basket, The, 55
Enchanted Spring, The (stage production), 25, 102
Enchanted Well, The, 55, 90
En marge de l'histoire de Cinématographe (text), 83
Ernst, Max, 62, 62
Eruption of Mount Pelee, The, 50, 51
Essanay Company, 67
Ethereal Suspension, The (illusion), 19
Every Man His Own Cigar Lighter, 58
Exploits and Opinions of Doctor Faustroll, The (novel), 120
Exposition Universelle (Paris, 1900), 42
Extraordinary Illusions, 93

Fairies' Dance, The (stage production), 38
Fairy of the Flowers, The (stage production), 22, 102
Fairyland, or the Kingdom of the Fairies, 58, 118
Fake-Diamond Swindler, A, 67
Fanfare (automaton), 17
Fantasmagorie (stage production), 37, 38
Fantastic Orange Tree, The (illusion), 19, 19
Farjaux (actor), 53
Faust, 81
Faust and Marguerite, 34, 58
Favart, Mme (actress), 14
Fée libellule, La, 68, 107, 107, 108
Fée Mab, La (conjuror), 22
Fernandez, José Fessi (fairground showman), 95
First Men in the Moon, The (novel), 51
Flea, The, 112
Fleischer, Max, 40
Floating Lady, The (illusion), 16
Florey, Robert, 103, 103n

Folies-Bergère, 53, 60, 72, 112
Folletto (conjuror), 22, 59
Ford, Francis (director), 74
Ford, John, 74, 127
Fornelio, M (tinter), 48
Fourier, Charles, 107, 119
Four Troublesome Heads, The, 37, 100
Fox, William, 67
Frégoligraphe, 42n
Frégoli illusionniste, 42n
Fregoli, Leopoldo, 42, 42n, 94n
Freud, Sigmund, 112
From the Earth to the Moon (novel), 51
Fuller, Loie (dancer), 96
Fulton, John P. (special effects specialist), 40
Fun With the Bridal Party, 68

Gagean, Émile (worker), 32
Galerie Vivienne (puppet-theatre in Paris), 18
Galipaux, Félix (actor), 18, 115
Gardener Burning Weeds, 29
Gare Montparnasse, 82, 83
Gaumont Company (Société Gaumont), 33, 72, 78, 79
Gaumont, Léon, 66, 71, 72, 73
General Film Company, 67
Génin, Eugénie (Méliès' first wife), 18, 81, 111
Georges Méliès (monograph), 10
Georges Méliès, créateur du spectacle cinématographique (monograph), 10
Georges Méliès, mage (monograph), 10
Ghosts Before Breakfast, 85
'Giant Swede', 'The' (artiste), 115, 115
Gill, André, 26
Gillet, Rachel (actress), 45, 60
Gilson, Paul (writer), 83, 92
Giraud (diplomat), 76
Golden Cage, The (stage production), 26
Gorilla Seizing a Young Girl (waxwork), 95
Goudeau, De (inventor), 33
Gounod, 58
Grand Café (Paris), 28
Grandmother's Story, 68, 69, 112
Grandville, J. J., 56
Griffe, La (satirical magazine), 26, 27
Grimault, Paul (producer), 85
Grivolas, Claude (businessman), 70, 94
Grooms, Red (artist), 52
Group L'Effort, 83
Gulledge, Jesse (actress), 74
Gulliver's Travels, 48

Guy, Alice (director), 79
Guyollot (custodian), 84

Habit ne fait pas le moine, L', 67
Haddock, William (manager), 74
Hallucinations du Baron de Münchausen, Les, 78
Halperin, Victor (director), 40
Hamlet, Prince of Denmark, 64
Hand of the Artist, The, 94n
Harmington (conjuror), 22, 23, 104n
Hasting, Jos (impresario), 72
Haunted Castle, The, 33
Hennegan & Co., 62
Henry, Émile (anarchist), 27
Hepworth, Cecil, 124
Histoire comparée du cinéma (comparative history), 10, 59n
Hommage à Méliès (collage), *108*
Hopkins, Albert Allis (writer), 36
Houdini, 63
Huizinga, Johan, 120
Human Fly, The, 51
Humanity Through the Ages, 67, 68
Hunting of the Snark, The (poem), 120
Hydrothérapie fantastique, 96
Hypnotism, Catalepsy, Magnetism (stage production), 23

Immortal Alamo, The, 73, *73*
Impossible Voyage, An, 58, *59*, 119, 120, *121*
Impressions of Africa (novel), 120
Incident From Don Quixote, 68
Indian Trunk, The (illusion), 81
Inexhaustible Bottle, The (illusion), 19
Ingres, 112
Inn Where No Man Rests, The, *91*
International Convention of Cinematograph Editors, 69, *70*
In The Bogie Man's Cave, 68
Invisible Man, The, 40, *40*, 46
Irritable Model, An, 113
Isola, Émile and Vincent (impresarios), 28, 58, 94
Isolatograph, 28

Jack Jaggs and Dum Dum, 56, 103
Jarry, Alfred, 67, 120
Javanese Dancers, 77
Jeanette's Wedding (comic-opera), 81
Jeanson, Henri (artiste), 81
Joan of Arc, 48
'Johnny the Cowboy', 76
Jupiter's Thunderbolts, 56

Kalem Company, 67
Kamenka, Alexander (director), 81
Keaton, Buster, 42
Kelm (actor), 53
Kétorza (fairground showman), 59n
Kineto, 94n
Kinétograph, 28, *28*, 30, 33, 95
Kinetoscope, 28, 71
King of the Sharpshooters, The, 101
Kleine, George (distributor), 67
Kolta, Buatier de (conjuror), 22, 30, 34, 108
Korsten, Lucien (mechanic), 28, 30
Kyrou, Ado, 97

Labial (automaton), 17
Labiche, Eugène (composer), 80
Laboratory of Mephistopheles, The, 33
Laemmle, Carl, 67
Lagrange, Louise (actress), 79, 80, 81
Lallement (worker), 35, 55
Landais (curator), 83
Landing of Members of the Congress, 29
Langlois, Henri, 85
Lapipe (mechanic), 28
Last Cartridges, The, 34
Last Moments of the Illustrious Poet Victor Hugo (waxwork), 95
Leborgne (friend), 30
Leclerc (cameraman), 22, 30, 33, 45
Leclerc, Mme, 22
Lecuit-Monroy (scenery-painter), 47
Legris (conjuror), 22, *23*, 59, *62*, *104*
Lemoine (criminal), 67
Lenne, Gérard (writer), 8, 127, 128
Lentiélectroplasticromomimocoliserpentographe, 95
Lévi-Strauss, Claude, 13
Library of Congress (Washington), 54
Life-Saving Up-to-Date, 60
Lightning Change Artiste, The, 42
Lilliputian Minuet, The, *18*, 90, 96
'Little Tich' (artiste), 115, *115*
Lo Duca, G. M. (historian), 10
Louvel (worker), 44
Lubin Company, 67
Lubin, Siegmund, 49
Lumière, Antoine, 28
Lumière, Louis, 28, *28*, 29, 30, 33, 34, 42, 42n, 71, 117

Magasin pittoresque, Le (humorous journal), 56
Magic Lantern, The, 56

Magic, Stage Illusions and Scientific Diversions, Including Trick Photography (book), 36, *37*
Maguire and Baucus, 53
Maison Lepère (store), 58
Maljournal (artiste), 81
Malthête-Méliès, Madeleine (historian), 10, 84, 97
Manet, 112
Manuel (director), 59
Man With the Rubber Head, The, 49, *50*, 98, *99*, *100*
Marbeau, Mme (artiste), 81
Marey, E.-J., 7
Marïen, Marcel (painter), *108*
Marinetti, F. T., 42n
Marquet, 117
'Marquis of O', 'The' (conjuror), 59
Marvellous Fishing (illusion), 19
Mary Queen of Scots, 34
Mary's Stratagem, *75*
Marx Brothers, 123
Maskelyne, John Nevil, 15, *16*, 17, 19, 20, 22, *25*, 40, 81, *90*, 101, 108, *111*
Maskelyne, Nevil, 20, 57, 94
Massacre in Crete, 34
Massé, Victor (composer), 81
Matho, Raymonde (artiste), 81
Mauclaire, J.-P. (cinéaste), 83
McLaren, Norman, 69n
Méliès (monograph), 10
Méliès, Adolphe (editor), 26
Méliès, André (artiste), 45, 81, 82
Méliès, François (artisan), 13
Méliès Gala, 83, *83*
Méliès, Gaston (director), 11, 13, 17, *48*, 49, 54, 61, 67, 72, *73*, 74, 76, 77, 78
Méliès, Georgette (artiste), 19, 35, 81, 82
Méliès, Henri (businessman), 13, 17, 49
Méliès, Louis (businessman), 13, *13*, 19, 35
Méliès Manufacturing Company, 67, 72, 73
Méliès, Paul (manager), 54, 72, 76, 78
Melomaniac, The, 37, 55, *56*, 93, *93*
Mendel, Georges (producer), 42
Merry Deeds of Satan, The (stage production), 62
Merry Frolics of Satan, The, 62, *63*, *92*, 97, 123
Mesguish, Félix (cameraman), 29
Mesmer, 23
Mesmerian Experiment, A, 60
Michaëlla (conjuror), 59
Michaut (cameraman), 31, 45, 55
Miller and the Sweep, The, 46
Minnie the Moocher, 40
Miracle Under the Inquisition, A, 112

Mirographe, 33, *33*
Mischievous Sketch, A, 64
Misfortunes of Mr and Mrs Mott on Their Trip to Tahiti, The, 76
Mishaps of the N.Y.–Paris Race, 67
Mitchell, Edmund (scriptwriter), 76
Monet, 117
Moon's Pranks, or the Misadventures of Nostradamus, The (stage production), 36, 114
Moreau, Gustave, 15
Morris, James (artiste), 98n
Motion Picture Patents Company (M.P.P.C.), 66, 67, 72, 74
Mottershaw, Frank (director), 124
Mounet-Sully (actor), 14
Mourguye, M and Mme (Eugénie Génin's guardians), 18
Mrs and Mr Duff, 72
Murder Will Out, 40
Musée des Arts Décoratifs (Paris), 10
Musée Grévin (Parisian waxworks), 34
Mutuelle du Cinéma (home for retired cinematographers), 84
Mysterious Island, The, 61
Mysterious Knight, The, 42
Mysterious Retort, The, 98

Natural Colour Kinematograph Company, 94n
Neptune and Amphitrite, 40
Neuville, Alfred de (painter), 34
Neuville, Alphonse de (illustrator), 64
New Death Penalty, A, 64
Nichols, Anne (actress), 74
Nicolodi, Mme (property owner), 82
Night With Masqueraders In Paris, A, 68
Nixon, Richard, 127
Nonguet, Lucien (director), 71
Notté, M (singer), 115
Nymph of the Fountain, The (painting), *109*

Odéon, Mme de l' (artiste), 81
Off to Bloomingdale Asylum (otherwise known as *Off to Bedlam*), 7, *35*, 45, *46*, 96
Okita (conjuror), 22
Olympia (painting), 112
Olympia (Parisian theatre), 72, 112
One-Man Band, The, 42
On The Comet, 64n
Opéra (Paris), 44, 115

Palace of the Arabian Nights, The, *41*, 118, *119*
Palais-Royal (Parisian theatre), 20

Paley, William (cameraman), 74
Panorama of Havre Taken From a Boat, 29
Papillon, Mlle Zizi (artiste), 56
Paris, Comte de, 26
Parvillier (scenery-painter), 47
Passez Muscade (revue), 42
Passion Considered As An Uphill Bicycle Race, The (novel), 120
Pastry-Cook of the Palais-Royal, The (automaton), 19
Pathé, Charles, 69, 71, 72, 78, *78*, 79, 80, 81, 112
Pathé Company (Société Pathé Frères), 33, 42, 48, 67, 70, 71, 72
Paul and Virginia (operetta), 81
Paul, R. W., 17, 28, *28*, 42n, 51, 94n
Paulus (singer), 26, 33, 33n
Pecci-Blunt, Count and Countess, 96n
Peeping Tom at the Seaside, A, 113
Pékin–Paris automobile en 80 jours (travelogue), 120
Pepper, John Henry, 38
Pepper's Ghost, 38, *39*
Péret, Benjamin, 93
Perrigot (cameraman), 29
Phantom of the Métro, The, 84
Phantoms of the Nile, The (pantomime), 72
Phantoms . . . R.I.P. (drawing), *128*
Phenakistiscope, 7
Philosopher's Stone, The, 98
Phrenologist and the Lively Skull, The, 47
Picabia, Francis, 127
'Ping Pongs', 'The' (artistes), 113
Pissarro, 117
Place de l'Opéra, The, 34
Plateau, Joseph (inventor), 7
Playhouse, The, 42
Playing Cards, 29
Poe, E. A., 40
Porter, Edwin S., 127
Praxinoscope, 7
Prévert, Jacques and Pierre, 85
Prolific Magical Egg, The, 50
Promio (cameraman), 29
Psycho (automaton), 17
Punch and Judy, 89, *90*
Pygmalion and Galatea, 100

Raft of the Medusa (waxwork), 95
Rains, Claude, 47
Ravachol (anarchist), 27
Ray, Man, 96n
Raynaly, E. (conjuror), 22, 26, 58, 59
Red Riding Hood, 45, *46*

Régie des Tabacs, La, *84*, 85
Rehm, M and Mme (artistes), 22
Renée, Mlle (artiste), 81
Resurrection of Cleopatra, The (illusion), 81
Reulos, Daniel (actor), 74, *74*, 75
Reulos, Lucien (businessman), 30, 33, 74, 95
Reynaud, Émile, 7
Richard, Jacques (historian), 10, 59n
Richter, Hans, 85
Rives, Jean (executor), 83
Robber of Angkor, The, 76
Robert-Houdin, Émile (conjuror), 19, *19*
Robert-Houdin, Jean-Eugène, 15, 19, *19*, 20, 21, 45, 59, 63, 83, 90, 98, 101
Robert-Houdin, Mme Émile, 82
Robert-Houdin's Portfolio (illusion), 19
Robert Macaire and Bertrand, *124*, *124*
Robertson, 37, 38, *38*
Robinson Crusoe, 22, *52*, 53, 59n
Rosay, Françoise (artiste), 81
Rouillon, Mme (tinter), 48
Rousseau, Henri, 57, 106
Roussel, Raymond, 95, 103, 120

Sadoul, Georges, 10, 36
Salle des Capucines (Paris), 45
Salle Pleyel (París), 83
Schuering, Johannah-Catherine (mother), 13
Sea Fighting in Greece, 34
Selig Company, 67
Sêmeuse, La (poem), *92*
Sennacherib in Two Parts and Screvins in Two Pieces (stage production), 16, *25*
Sérénades de Frégoli, Les, 42n
Seurat, 117
Seven Capital Sins, The, 43, *43*
Shakespeare Writing 'Julius Caesar', 64
Shoot the Moon, *52*
Skeleton Dance, The, 40, *41*
Skipping Cheeses, The, 63
'Smile', 'Geo', 26, 27
Smith, George A., 46
'Snow Drops', 'The' (artistes), 60
Snow Queen, The (story), 108
Soap Bubbles, 62
Société Française de Photographie et de Cinématographie, 69
Sophos, the Domino Player (automaton), 19
Sphinx of the Icefields, The (story), 79
Spirit Case or Mrs. Daffodil Downey's Light and Dark Seance, A (stage production), 16, *39*, 40

Spirit Phenomena (stage production), *23*, 62, *62*, 72
Spiritualistic Photographer, A, 56, *90*
Star Film, 30, 42, 49, 53, 54, 61, 70, 74, 78, 79, 83, 92, 98, 103, 106, 108, 113, 114, 122
Star Film Agency, 49
Star Film Catalogue, 42, 62, 114, 124
Star Film Ranch, 73
Star Film Trading Company, 62n, 66
Stichel, Mme (choreographer), 64
Stolen Wireless, The, 72
Storey, Edith (actress), 74, *75*
Storey, Francis (actor), 74
Stuart, Gloria (actress), *40*
Studio 28 (Parisian ciné-club), 83
Supermale, The (novel), 67, 120
Surgeon, The (silhouette), 26
Surprising Silk Handkerchief, The (trick), 19

Taillis, Jean du (writer), 120
Tainguy, P. (manager), 72, *73*
Talazac (conjuror), 59
Tell Tale Hat, The, 16
Temptation of Saint Anthony, The (stage production), 38
Temptation of Saint Anthony, The, 36, 110, *110*
Terrible Night, A, 120
Thanking the Audience, 43
Théâtre des Variétés-Artistiques (Montreuil), 81
Théâtre Le Peletier (Paris), 93
Théâtre Robert-Houdin (Paris), 19, 20, *20*, *21*, 22, 26, 28, 30, 32, 33, 36, 42, 43, 58, 71, 80, 82, 93, 96, 103n
Three Graces Changed Into Skeletons, The (stage production), 38
Thuillier, Mme (tinter), 47, 48
Tissot, Alice (artiste), 81
Tit For Tat, or a Good Joke With My Head, 100
Todorov, Tzvetan (writer), 106
Tosca (operetta), 81
Tourtin (photographer), 45
Tower of London, The, *44*
Tracy, Irene (actress), 76
Treasures of Satan, The, 87, *88*
Trewey, Felicien, 94
Triple Lady, The, 37
Trip to the Moon, A (puppet show), 95
Trip to the Moon, A, 36, 51, *51*, *52*, 53, 103, 120
Troupe Raymond, 33
Tunnelling the English Channel, 48, *122*, 123
Twenty Thousand Leagues Under the Sea (novel), 64, *65*, 120

Uccello, Paolo, 87n

U.K. Kineplastikon Films, 94n
Under the Seas, 64, *65*, 122
Undressing of the Model, The, 112
Unwilling Cowboy, An, 74
Upside Down, 51
Up-to-Date Mountebank, An (stage production), 25, 102
Up-to-Date Surgery, 51, 103
Urban, Charles, 53, *53*, 54

Vaillant (anarchist), 27
Vallouy, Mme (tinter), 48
Vanishing Lady, The (illusion), 30, *30*, 34, 108
Variétés (Parisian theatre), 112
Velle, Gaston (director), 71, 94
Venus Cajoling a Hermit (stage production), 38
Verne, Jules, 51, 64, 64n, 79, 119, 120
Vidal (murderer), 95
View of the Wreck of the 'Maine', A, 36
Vitagraph Corporation, 67, 76, 78
Vitrail diabolique, Le, 78
Voisin, Émile (theatrical supplier), 17, 22
Voyage de la famille Bourrichon, Le, 80

Wandering Jew, The, 123, *123*
War Episodes, 34
Warwick Film Catalogue, 113
Warwick Trading Company, 53
Watering Flowers, 29
Wells, H. G., 51
Westcar Papyrus, 101
Western Studio (California), 74, *74*
Whale, James, 40, 46, 47
While Under the Hypnotist's Influence, 112
White Zombie, 40
Who Looks, Pays, 61
Williamson, James (director), 124
Witch, The, 62
Wonderful Invention, The, 64n
Wonderful Living Fan, The, *109*

Xour Lotion, 36

Yacht Race (Reliance–Shamrock III), The, 54
Yellow Dwarf, The (stage production), *23*
Yellow Slave, The, 76, *77*
Yermoliev, Joseph (director), 81

Zach the Hermit (stage production), 16
Zecca, Ferdinand, 71, *78*, 79, 80
Zeman, Karel, 64n
Zirka (conjuror), 59
Zoe (automaton), 17